THE
JEWISH-AMERICAN
ANSWER BOOK

The Ethnic Answer Books

The African-American Answer Book
The German-American Answer Book
The Irish-American Answer Book
The Jewish-American Answer Book

The Ethnic Answer Books

THE JEWISH-AMERICAN ANSWER BOOK

Ellen Shnidman

General Editors

Sandra Stotsky
Harvard Graduate School of Education

Reed Ueda
Tufts University

Chelsea House Publishers • Philadelphia

CHELSEA HOUSE PUBLISHERS

Editor in Chief: Stephen Reginald
Managing Editor: James D. Gallagher
Production Manager: Pamela Loos
Art Director: Sara Davis
Picture Editor: Judy L. Hasday
Senior Production Editor: Lisa Chippendale
Associate Art Director: Takeshi Takahashi
Designer: Keith Trego
Editorial Assistants: Anne Hill, Heather Forkos
Picture Research: Lillian Mittleman

The Chelsea House World Wide Web site address is
www.chelseahouse.com

First Printing

1 3 5 7 9 8 6 4 2

Library of Congress Cataloging-in-Publication Data

The Jewish-American answer book / Ellen Schnidman ;
general editors,
Sandra Stotsky, Reed Ueda.
p. cm. — (The ethnic answer books)
Includes bibliographical references (p.)
Summary: Presents questions covering the history, culture
and social life, religion, political activities, economic life, and
accomplishments of Jewish Americans, with a separate
section of answers.

ISBN 0-7910-4799-7 (hc)
ISBN 0-7910-4800-4 (pb)

1. Jews—United States—Miscellanea—Juvenile literature.
2. Questions and answers—Juvenile literature. [1. Jews—
United States—Miscellanea. 2. Questions and answers.] I.
Stotsky, Sandra. II. Ueda, Reed. III. Schnidman, Ellen.
Ethnic answer books.
E184.35.J49 1999
973' .04924—dc21   98-35850
                                                          CIP
                                                          AC

CONTENTS

Introduction
ETHNIC ANSWER BOOKS

O ver half a century ago, Louis Adamic, a Slovenian immigrant who had become a popular writer, described the United States as a country "all of a piece, a blend of cultures from many lands, woven of threads from many corners of the world." The history of the United States shows that this nation has indeed been woven from many strands. More immigrants and more ethnic groups have come to live in America than in any other country in the world. In fact, the United States has been the most powerful magnet for international migration in world history.

Extensive immigration began in the 17th century when English settlers began to colonize North America, intermingling with the early Dutch settlers as well as the indigenous peoples of this continent. Blacks also came in large numbers, imported from Africa to serve as slaves. Well before the American Revolution, other groups of people—the Germans, French Huguenots, Scots, Welsh, and Scotch-Irish were the major groups—also began to migrate here. After the American Revolution, the United States' favorable immigration policies led to a large influx of immigrants, who helped settle and develop the new country. From 1820 to 1930, 38,000,000 people moved to the United States while 24,000,000 people migrated to Canada, Argentina, Brazil, Australia, New Zealand, South Africa, and other areas. From World War II to the early 1990s, 20,000,000 newcomers flocked to the United States. As a result of these continuous waves of migration to America's shores, the United States and Canada have evolved into multi-ethnic countries of remarkable proportions, with each having absorbed an enormous variety of ethnic groups.

Educators at all levels are now encouraging greater attention to the many dimensions of American diversity, especially our religious and ethnic diversity. As a part of their study of American history, students are now being asked to learn about the Irish, Italians, Chinese, Poles, Mexicans, and Germans—to name some of our country's major immigrant ethnic groups—as well as the African Americans and the indigenous peoples of this continent. Indeed, the distinctive characteristics and contributions of all this country's ethnic groups have now taken a place at the center of our school curriculum.

This new series of educational texts seeks to provide secondary students with a handy and compact reference work they can use to learn how a democratic nation was built out of intermixture and interdependence. All the volumes in this series are similar in three important respects. Every volume has a question and answer format. Each book supplies a core of factual information about a particular ethnic group. And all the volumes are organized by common chapters.

The creators of this series have designed this format to accomplish several educational goals. First, we offer questions about key features of the group's life and history in order to arouse students' curiosity about this particular group of Americans. Questions also serve to provide models of inquiry for students; these are the kinds of questions a historian asks when seeking to understand the history and life of a group of people. Second, the answers we provide to these questions are designed to yield a nucleus of significant facts. These facts can be drawn on for research reports, and they can serve as a point of departure for further inquiry into the history and experiences of an ethnic group. Finally, all the questions are organized into common chapters across all books in the series so that students can make informative comparisons and contrasts among American ethnic groups.

The first two chapters in each volume deal with the group's origins and arrival in America. The next three chapters provide information on the group's economic, religious, and social life and institutions in this country. Another three chapters present information on the group's distinctive characteristics, intellectual and cultural life, and participation in American public life. The final chapter describes important or accomplished individuals in this group's history in America. By comparing and contrasting information in these chapters among various ethnic groups, students have an excellent opportunity to learn about many significant features of American life, both in the past and today. They can learn about the different ways that each group has drawn on America's political principles and institutions to integrate its members into American political life. They can discover the different ways that America's ethnic groups interacted with each other as well as with the descendants of the English settlers who framed this country's political principles and institutions. They can find out how members of each group took advantage of this country's free public schools and free public libraries to advance themselves socially, intellectually, and economically. And students can begin to understand the remarkable similarities in the experiences of many ethnic groups in this country despite their having come from many different parts of the world, as well as the remarkable differences among ethnic groups who have come from the same parts of the world.

It is our hope that this series of books will serve as an intellectual guidepost to further student learning. It will help supply a solid foundation of knowledge that students can draw on to supplement what they learn in their classes on American history, literature, and government. And students will learn how to ask "good" questions about ethnicity. They will learn from the answers that it is a subject full of surprises and complexity—that ethnicity is not equivalent to race or language, that an ethnic group's characteristics depend heavily on when large numbers of its members arrive in this country, and that a group's characteristics change markedly from generation to generation in America. As a result, students will find the study of ethnic history a fascinating experience of discovery about how this country became the most successful democracy in history.

—Sandra Stotsky and Reed Ueda

Foreword
THE JEWISH AMERICANS

I n many places, the history of the Jewish people is by and large tragic. This is not the case in America. In the early 20th century, Jewish immigrants from Eastern Europe called America the *goldene medina*, the golden country. While this image doesn't match the experiences of many first- and second-generation immigrants, it does express what Jews as a group have experienced since they first arrived in America in 1654.

America is the first country the Jews have lived in (other than their homeland Israel) where they have enjoyed civic equality and individual rights similar to other citizens. In spite of some continuing prejudice (or anti-Semitism) on the part of individuals, and some past discrimination by institutions, Jewish Americans have enjoyed a freedom to pursue their dreams that is unparalleled in any other place or time. The first Jews to arrive in America in the 17th century were Sephardic. They were the descendants of Jews who had been expelled from Spain and Portugal in the 15th century. In the middle of the 19th century came a larger wave of German Jews. Then at the end of the 19th century, an enormous group of Eastern European Jews arrived in America. This last group has largely dominated the culture and tone of American Jewish life during this century. Smaller groups of Syrian, Iranian, and Israeli Jews, as well as a large group of Soviet Jews, have been added to the mix in the second half of the 20th century.

The record of Jewish accomplishment in America is impressive. Starting in the 17th and 18th centuries, almost all Jews who came to America brought nothing but talent, ambition, and community ties. Yet they were able to establish themselves quickly in business and in professions. Eastern European Jews improved their economic status in a remarkably short period of time, although at first most of them labored in sweatshops and lived in poverty. The small shopkeepers and factory workers who made up the majority of Jewish immigrants have faded into history. Their descendants include professionals, business executives, artists, and politicians. Jewish Americans prospered economically as America prospered. They have the highest average household income of all American subgroups. Like other immigrant groups from Europe, most Jews settled in the major cities of the Northeast and Midwest from 1850 to 1925. The traditional Judaism of the small towns of Central and Eastern Europe was transformed in America into three major branches: Orthodox, Conservative, and Reform Judaism. The language that most Jewish immigrants spoke—Yiddish—eventually disappeared from daily speech except among the Hasidim. However, its influence is seen in American slang expressions.

Although rarely more than three percent of the American population, Jews have left a deep mark on America's popular culture and intellectual life. In the early 20th century, involvement in musical entertainment and comedy in major northeastern cities (especially New York) became a trademark of second-generation Jews. Broadway musical theater and the Hollywood film industry were largely created by Jews. Jewish immigrants from Europe left a culture that respected learning and held the scholar in highest esteem. This value is reflected in the disproportionate number of Jews in professions such as medicine, law, academia, and intellectual life. Many of America's most prominent writers and musicians have been Jews. This is true of both Jews who immigrated, such as Isaac Bashevis Singer and Vladimir Horowitz, and those born in the U.S., such as Bernard Malamud and Leonard Bernstein. One-quarter of America's Nobel Prize winners in this century are Jewish. Jewish Americans translated a love of ideas into an affection for ideologies. Many of the major political ideologies and social theories of 20th-century America were developed by Jews. The Jewish community itself engages in changing but continuous internal debate about political, cultural, and religious issues. Jewish immigrants to America found a society where individual effort and merit were rewarded. To strengthen and insure this commitment to equal treatment under the law, Jewish Americans have been at the forefront of the civil rights movement. They have offered strong support to groups promoting civil liberties and cultural diversity.

Since its establishment in 1948, the nation of Israel has loomed large in the consciousness of the American Jewish community. Fund-raising activities and political lobbying on Israel's behalf have engaged the energies of community leaders, both religious and secular, over the last 50 years. This interest in Israel as well as involvement in activities to keep people aware of the Holocaust—the slaughter of European Jews by the Nazis in World War II—have largely defined Jewish institutional life since the 1940s.

Concerns about anti-Semitism and social exclusion dominated Jewish community life for several generations. These issues have given way to fears that young people marrying those of other faiths and blending in with American culture will erode the Jewish community. Jews in America do not face a hostile culture that uses them as scapegoats for its problems. Instead the American Jewish community lives in a tolerant society. Individualism is the dominant creed, and ethnic immigrant communities largely disappear by the third or fourth generation.

Today the focus of community life has shifted to strengthening the Jewish family, religious education, and the overall fabric of Jewish culture. In the past, Jewish community life was defined by concerns about political causes and interfaith relations. Now it is increasingly defined by the differences between liberal, secular Jews and more conservative, religious ones. Because anti-Semitic attacks have decreased and Israel's continued existence seems less threatened, the internal divisions of the American Jewish community are becoming the largest item on their agenda. If current trends continue, the religious population will grow and the secular population will shrink. The American Jewish community of the future is likely to be smaller, more politically conservative, and more traditional in its religious practices.

—Ellen Shnidman

Questions

◀ The Hebrew prophet Moses leads the Hebrews across the Red Sea, away from their lives of slavery in Egypt. According to the Bible, Moses received the Ten Commandments, laws that are an integral part of the Jewish faith, from God while leading the Israelites through the desert to the "promised land," Canaan. This woodcut is from the Gutenberg Bible.

CHAPTER

1

ORIGINS

Antiquity

1-1 Who is considered the first Jew? When and how did he arrive in Israel?

1-2 Who are the Patriarchs of the Jewish people?

1-3 Who are the Matriarchs of the Jewish people?

1-4 When did the Jews settle in Israel, and what caused them to leave?

1-5 When did the ancient Israelites (or Jews) return to Israel?

1-6 When and how did Judaism become the official religion of the Israelites?

1-7 According to the Bible, the ancient Israelites conquered Canaan (Israel) by force under the leadership of Joshua. Some current theories suggest a different view of what happened. What is this view?

1-8 The Jews were the first people in recorded history to worship one God (monotheism). What other monotheistic faiths evolved from Judaism?

1-9 Under what king did ancient Israel have its largest historical boundaries?

1-10 The Babylonians conquered Israel in 586 B.C. and destroyed the great temple that Solomon had built in Jerusalem. What movement in Jewish history did this event begin?

1-11 Part of the Jewish population that went into exile in Babylon returned to Israel, or Zion, in the sixth century B.C. (beginning 538 B.C.) What allowed the Jews to return?

1-12 What did the returning Jewish exiles do to mark their return to Zion?

1-13 For how long has the land of Israel been considered the center of the Jewish people in the world?

1-14 Which communities outside Israel were the most important from the sixth century B.C. until the time of Jesus?

1-15 After A.D. 135, most Jews lived outside Israel. What was the major cause of this dispersion?

Middle Ages

1-16 The major Jewish communities of the Diaspora in Europe were established during the first millennium (A.D. 0–1000). Jewish communities in the Middle East date back to 1000 B.C. How did Judaism sustain itself as a rather uniform faith when most of its followers were scattered over so many different places?

1-17 In addition to the Jewish community in Israel, other distinct Jewish communities in the Middle East date back to 1000 B.C. Where were these communities located?

1-18 What are the two major groups into which the worldwide Jewish population has been divided for the past one thousand years?

1-19 Why did the center of Jewish population move from Spain and Central Europe to Eastern Europe between the 9th and 16th centuries A.D.?

1-20 During the Middle Ages (A.D. 500–1500) the Christians of Europe increased discrimination toward their Jewish neighbors. While there were times in particular countries, such as Spain, when Jews held political power, generally they were looked on with suspicion. Many times spontaneous riots against Jews or planned persecution by governments led to Jews being killed. With so much hatred being directed against the Jews, why did Christians allow them to continue living in Europe?

1-21 During the Golden Age of Islam (8th–13th centuries A.D.) the Sephardic Jews of the Arab world made major contributions to its economic and cultural renaissance. Who was the most important Jewish intellectual figure during this period?

1-22 How did the conditions of the Jewish communities of the Arab world differ from those in Europe during the Middle Ages?

Modern Europe

1-23 On July 12, 1555, Pope Paul IV issued a decree introducing a concept that had a great impact on the next four hundred years of Jewish history. What was the decree, and what concept did it introduce?

1-24 Which European philosopher of Jewish origin helped lay the foundations for modern skeptical (or rationalist) attitudes toward religion?

1-25 During the 18th century in Eastern Europe, a mystical religious movement known as Hasidism swept through the Jewish population. At its peak in the mid-19th century, Hasidism included about half of the Jews of Eastern Europe. Hasidic groups formed around charismatic leaders known as rebbes. What was the name of the rabbi who founded the Hasidic movement, and what was unique about his approach to religious life?

1-26 During the 19th century, the Jews of Eastern Europe lived mainly under the rule of the Russian czars. What were the policies of the czars toward Jewish settlement?

1-27 Meanwhile, the French Revolution ushered in a period of liberalization in Western Europe. Jews were granted civil rights they had never enjoyed before. They were able to move outside their neighborhoods and participate more fully in the political and economic life of Western European countries. What prime minister of mid-19th century England was a baptized Jew?

1-28 The secularization of Western European society in the 18th and 19th centuries allowed Jews to be accepted as equal citizens. What development in the 19th and 20th centuries dashed the hopes of Jews for social equality in Europe?

1-29 During the 19th century, the Jewish population of the world (the great bulk of it in Europe) grew from roughly 2 million to 11 million. What factors contributed to this population explosion?

1-30 This population explosion was partly to blame for the poverty and high unemployment in the Jewish towns and villages of Eastern Europe. It also made the Jews more visible in the general population and led to increased persecution. How did the Jews react to this situation?

1-31 Most Jews in America come from Eastern European shtetls (little towns), made famous by the musical and movie *Fiddler on the Roof.* The three character types used in the play to symbolize shtetl life were the rabbi, the matchmaker, and the beggar. What did these characters represent?

1-32 Roughly one-third of the Jews living in Eastern Europe left that region between 1880 and 1925. To which countries did most of these Jews move?

1-33 In modern times, European society became polarized between conservative (or reactionary) and liberal (or progressive) forces. Which of these two movements did most Jews support? Why?

1-34 Between 1800 and 1970, the Jews of the Islamic world lived in deteriorating political and social conditions. Why was this the case?

1-35 In the 20th century, two totalitarian movements succeeded in coming to power in Europe. Both of these regimes were anti-Semitic (against Jews). They crushed what existed of Jewish community life in most of Europe. Identify the two regimes and explain why they were anti-Semitic.

1-36 By 1933, with the rise of Hitler and the Nazi Party to power in Germany, the situation of the Jews in continental Europe became desperate. Because most of their families had lived in Europe for more than 1,000 years, many Jews could not imagine fleeing to another continent. Nor were most of them interested in becoming pioneers and settling in Palestine, which was a threatened and underdeveloped society. Why couldn't they move to the United States?

1-37 The Evian Conference in July 1938 was organized to discuss the plight of Jewish refugees fleeing Nazi persecution. What was the result of this conference?

1-38 During the desperate months of 1939, the U.S. State Department sought unsuccessfully to find destinations for Jewish refugees fleeing Nazi-occupied Europe. Where were some of the places they considered using as refugee settlements?

1-39 The state of Israel was established in 1948, three years after the end of World War II. The main factor that allowed the nation to come into existence was the courage and steadfastness of the 600,000 Jews living there on the eve of the 1948 War of Independence. What factor was important in securing political recognition for the new state?

The Contemporary World

1-40 What are the different names that have been given to the Jewish people throughout history?

1-41 As a result of World War II and the Holocaust, the distribution of the Jewish population of the Diaspora has drastically changed. What are the main centers of Jewish life outside of Israel today?

1-42 During the biblical period, probably 80 percent of Jews lived in Israel and 20 percent in small communities out-side Palestine. By the year 1600, only 1 percent of Jews lived in Israel. Only in the last century has there been a major change in these statistics. Why has the proportion of Jews living in Israel increased dramatically?

1-43 The Jewish community of the United States is the largest, wealthiest, and most influential community in the Diaspora today and probably in the history of the Jewish people. What other historical Jewish communities could be compared to it?

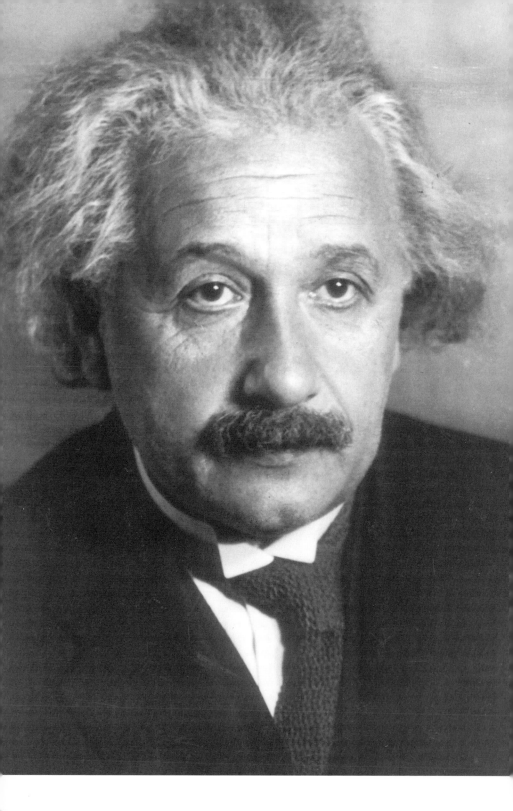

◀ Albert Einstein, a German-born Jew, won the Nobel prize for physics in 1921. His theories of relativity, gravitation, and unified fields made him the most renowned scientist of the early 20th century. German Jews were among the first wave of Jewish immigrants to the United States and were a large part of the established American Jewish community at the turn of the century. Einstein became an American citizen in 1940.

ARRIVAL IN AMERICA

Waves of Immigration

2-1 How many distinct waves of Jewish immigrants came to America?

2-2 The first Jews to come to America during the 17th century were mostly Sephardic. Where did they come from?

2-3 Where did these Sephardic Jews settle?

2-4 By the middle of the 18th century, Jews were able to participate in some aspects of public life in many of the 13 colonies. The Protestant majority often welcomed or tolerated their presence more readily than they welcomed Catholic immigrants. Why?

2-5 When was the first major wave of Jewish immigration to America, and where did these Jews come from?

2-6 What drove the immigration of Jews from Europe between 1850 and 1925?

2-7 American anti-Semitism, where it existed, was never as lethal and destructive as European anti-Semitism. What characterized European anti-Semitism?

2-8 How was American anti-Semitism different from European hostility?

2-9 The flood of Jewish immigration from Eastern Europe began in 1881 and continued unchecked until the American government established immigration restrictions in 1924. What four main events occurred in Russia during that period which unleashed this wave of immigration?

2-10 Other than economic opportunity and freedom from persecution, what attracted Eastern European Jews to American life?

2-11 The 104,000 German Jews who entered the United States from 1933 to 1941 were the best educated immigrant population that ever came to America. What are they credited with accomplishing in American universities after World War II?

2-12 The Institute for Advanced Study at Princeton University was established in 1933, mainly by Jewish philanthropy, to accommodate German-Jewish scholars fleeing Hitler. Who was one of its first and most famous appointees?

2-13 The Syrian Jews who came to America after 1948 did not adapt to American culture in the same way as did most of the European Ashkenazi Jews. In what ways were the Syrian Jews different?

2-14 Since 1948, several hundred thousand Israeli citizens have permanently immigrated to the United States. Why have they decided to live in America?

2-15 The communist regime in the Soviet Union pursued many anti-Semitic policies. Given its hostile attitude toward

Jews, why did it refuse to allow any large Jewish emigration until the 1970s?

2-16 In what ways do the Soviet Jews who have come to America in the last 25 years differ from most previous groups of Jewish immigrants?

2-17 New immigrants from the former Soviet Union have a very different political orientation than the Jews who came from Russia between 1870 and 1924. How do the political views of the new wave of Russian Jews differ from the old wave?

2-18 A wave of immigration from Iran (30,000–50,000 people) began around 1979 and has continued sporadically since then. What caused the Iranian Jewish community to leave Iran after living there for 2500 years?

Settlement in America

2-19 What did George Washington write to the Jewish community of Newport, Rhode Island, in 1790?

2-20 Which American city was the major port of entry for Jews coming from Europe in the 19th and 20th centuries?

2-21 New York has become one of the great centers of Jewish life in the last 150 years. Even second- and third-generation Jews from other parts of America have flocked to New York for education and work. It has been said that the two cities most loved by Jews in the 20th century are Jerusalem and New York. Why New York?

2-22 The first neighborhood in New York City made up of both Jews and African Americans dates back to the beginning of the 20th century. What was the name of this neighborhood, and what has happened to it during the last 100 years?

2-23 In 1960, one-half of American Jews lived in and around New York City. Most of the rest lived in industrial areas in the Northeast and Midwest. Where is the Jewish population concentrated today?

2-24 The Jewish community of Los Angeles is the second largest in the United States. What initially caused Jews to move to Los Angeles from the eastern ports?

2-25 From 1948 to 1958, fair-housing laws were passed by many states and upheld by the U.S. Supreme Court. How did this affect the Jews?

2-26 After World War II, most American Jews, along with many other second- and third-generation Americans, moved to suburbs outside major cities. Unlike many other ethnic or religious groups, Jews settled in their own neighborhoods in the suburbs, rather than scattering throughout the area. They often settled in towns that had previously been inhabited by upper-middle-class and upper-class Protestant Americans. Why did Jews settle in these towns?

2-27 Can you give examples of suburbs outside major cities that went from being the homes of primarily affluent Protestants to being the homes of primarily affluent Jews?

2-28 Before World War II, property laws prevented Jews from settling in most of Miami Beach. After the war, these laws were eliminated. Jews quickly became a majority of the population in Miami Beach. Then in the 1980s, another group of immigrants appeared in Miami Beach. Who was this group of immigrants?

2-29 Small Jewish communities in southern and plains states were established in the late 19th and early 20th centuries. Many of these communities are now dying. Why is this happening?

Problems with Immigration to America

Although today the United States boasts one of the largest Jewish populations in the world, there has not always been a positive atmosphere for the expansion of the Jewish community in America. A genuine crisis arose with the fight over immigration laws in the first half of 20th century.

Immigration was strictly controlled in the United States in the 1930s and 1940s, with specific limits placed on the number of people allowed into America from different countries around the world. With the rise of Nazi persecution of Jews in Europe in the 1930s, there was a great need for the United States to allow more immigration of Jewish refugees from Eastern Europe. But a combination of anti-Semitic feeling and a desire not to get involved in the conflict on the part of many Americans served to block all efforts to loosen the rigid immigration policies.

Many efforts to change immigration law were particularly creative, if not successful. In 1941, a bill allowing 20,000 German Jewish children into America failed to pass. Another suggested plan that failed would have opened only Alaska to Jewish immigration.

Even as advocates worked to change the laws, many officials responded by placing more restrictions on Jewish immigration. Visas, or immigration passes into the United States, became more and more difficult to receive because of new complicated procedures imposed by the State Department. As a result of these new regulations, the quota for Jewish immigrants was not fulfilled in the early 1940s, despite the number of Jews fleeing the terror of Europe. ▪

◄ Jewish immigrants made a living in a number of ways once they arrived in America. Jews became heavily involved in the garment industry, and they were largely responsible for organizing the many garment labor unions that sprang up in the late 19th and early 20th centuries.

CHAPTER

3

ECONOMIC LIFE

3-1 What were the three industries or businesses that Jewish immigrants to America specialized in and became associated with in the early 20th century?

3-2 Most Jewish immigrants who came to America in the late 19th and early 20th centuries started out in the working class. They labored in sweatshops and factories, particularly in the needle trades (the clothing industry). What distinguished this group of immigrants from many others who worked in similar occupations?

3-3 Shmuel Gelbfisz (later known as Samuel Goldwyn) was like many Jewish immigrants of his generation. He started out in the clothing industry as a glove salesman in Gloversville, New York. Where did he later move?

3-4 The first predominantly Jewish labor union was the International Ladies Garment Worker's Union (ILGWU). It was founded in 1900. What was this union known for?

3-5 Levi Strauss, famous for making jeans, started his business in San Francisco in the middle of the 19th century. Why did he produce very durable trousers?

3-6 What are some of the major financial institutions in New York City that were founded by German-Jewish families?

3-7 What are three examples of large department stores founded or developed by Jews?

3-8 What innovation in home building did William Levitt make after World War II?

3-9 It used to be said that you couldn't buy good-tasting bagels outside of New York City. Nowadays, high quality bagels can be found all over America. Who introduced bagels as a mass-market food?

3-10 How did Meyer Lansky and Benjamin "Bugsy" Siegel achieve notoriety?

3-11 David Sarnoff came to America at the age of nine and later went on to head the company that developed radio as the first electronic mass-communication medium. What was that company?

3-12 Developed by Vladimir Zworykin, a Russian-Jewish immigrant, and refined by RCA and its subsidiary, the National Broadcasting Company (NBC), what mass-communication device would become perhaps the most important invention of the 20th century?

3-13 After World War II, Edwin Land founded a corporation that produced the instant camera. What was the name of this corporation?

3-14 Polio epidemics were one of the most feared health hazards after World War II. Who were the two scientists of Jewish background who developed vaccines that ended these epidemics?

3-15 The American publishing industry, like most other

industries, was dominated by Protestant Americans until after World War II. Name several publishing companies founded by Jews that have become dominant in the industry during the last 50 years.

3-16 In German-speaking nations of Central Europe during the 19th and early 20th centuries, Jews owned and edited some of the most prominent newspapers. In America, the son of a German-Jewish immigrant assumed the ownership of a struggling newspaper in 1896. It later became the most prestigious newspaper in the nation. Who was the man, and what was the newspaper?

3-17 The first Jew to become a major force in American journalism was Joseph Pulitzer. During the mid–19th century, he succeeded in producing mass-circulation newspapers that appealed to popular tastes. What is he most known for today?

3-18 Many of America's top lawyers and legal scholars have been Jews. What two Jewish professors who taught at Harvard Law School have achieved great fame?

3-19 Throughout the past century, American Jews have been known for their willingness to give to philanthropic causes. Which Jewish charity is consistently ranked in the top five among all American charities for the amount of money raised?

3-20 In the late 1980s, what proportion of America's practicing psychiatrists were Jews?

3-21 Why did such a high proportion of Jews join professions that require scholarly or intellectual ability?

◀ The Torah (the first five books of the Hebrew Bible) is a key text of Jewish wisdom and law. The Torah's teachings and beliefs are central to Judaism and extremely important to the Jewish people. It is a tradition among Sephardic Jews to keep Torah scrolls in elaborate cases, such as this one.

CHAPTER

4

RELIGIOUS LIFE

Religious Beliefs

4-1   How did Judaism differ from other religions of antiquity?

4-2   The central concept of the Jewish faith is that of the covenant between God and the Jewish people. With whom in particular was this covenant made?

4-3   An important difference between Judaism and Christianity is the Jewish emphasis on the present life over the afterlife. Is there a belief in an afterlife in Judaism?

4-4   One of the most important fundamentals of Judaism is the belief in the sanctity of human life and the equality of all people before God. Why is this idea so important?

4-5   The central book of the Jewish theology is called the Torah (the first five books of the Old Testament or Hebrew Bible). What period of Jewish history does the Torah describe?

4-6   The cornerstone of the Jewish faith is the Ten Commandments. What are they?

4-7 What is the traditional Jewish view of the Messianic Age?

4-8 What is the Talmud?

4-9 One of the most powerful parts of the Hebrew Bible (Old Testament) are sections from the prophets. What was the role of the prophets?

4-10 One of the religious thinkers most popular with contemporary traditional Jews is the medieval Sephardic rabbi and philosopher Maimonides. Why is he is so popular?

4-11 Why has Jerusalem been the most important and holy city in the Jewish faith since David made it the capital of Israel three thousand years ago?

4-12 There are a number of symbols associated with Judaism. The most popular is the Star of David, a six-pointed star. What is the origin of this emblem?

4-13 The other main symbol associated with the Jewish people is the menorah (candelabra). This is one of the official symbols of modern Israel. In Roman times an engraving of a candelabra was included in the arch of Titus in Rome, built in A.D. 81. What did this engraving memorialize?

4-14 Almost all holidays on the Jewish calendar began during biblical times (2,000 to 4,000 years ago). However, two holidays have been added during the last 50 years. What are they?

4-15 What are the three most important holidays in the Jewish calendar (as celebrated in America), and what is their significance?

4-16 In a traditional Jewish community, life revolves around the observance of the Sabbath. What are the important observances that set the Sabbath apart?

4-17 What are the Jewish dietary laws known as Kashrut (keeping kosher)?

4-18 Passover celebrates the exodus of Hebrew slaves from Egypt and their freedom from bondage. What did Moses and the Hebrews do and where did they go after they left Egypt?

4-19 Passover is a holiday that has special dietary requirements. What is the main requirement?

4-20 The holiday of Hannukah commemorates the victory of the Maccabees in ancient Israel over the Greeks who were trying to stamp out the practice of Judaism (164 B.C.). What is the miracle that is celebrated on this holiday?

Customs and Modern Adaptations

4-21 What religious item is placed on the right doorpost of a traditional Jewish home? What does it contain?

4-22 Where are the scrolls of the Torah placed inside a synagogue?

4-23 The ark in a synagogue is supposed to face the east. Why?

4-24 When Jewish boys turn 13 years old and Jewish girls turn 12 years old, they participate in a religious ceremony recognizing that child as an adult member of the Jewish community. This ceremony consists of reading a section from the prophets in the weekly Torah reading and a discussion of the meaning of the reading as part of the weekly Sabbath service. What is the name of this ceremony?

4-25 What are the three main branches of Judaism in contemporary America, and what distinguishes each group?

4-26 Why do religious Jews tend to be socially and politically more conservative than secular Jews?

4-27 The Reform and Modern Orthodox branches of Judaism have established themselves as uniquely American brands of Judaism. What makes them unique in the 4000-year history of Judaism?

Recent Trends

4-28 During the 1960s, the Reform branch of Judaism emphasized political involvement and devotion to liberal social causes as an important part of its philosophy. Which social cause of that decade were they closely associated with?

4-29 In the last 20 years, how has the religious role of women changed in the more liberal branches of Judaism (Reform and Conservative)?

4-30 Recently the Reform movement has started to emphasize the importance of tradition, observance of some rituals, and study of the Bible and the Hebrew language. Why have these changes occurred?

4-31 Starting in the 1960s, a small group of Jews made efforts to incorporate aspects of the counterculture into Jewish community life. Many of these attempts did not produce any lasting result. However, some have endured. What is one example of this?

4-32 A well-known rabbi and Jewish folksinger launched his own outreach movement in the late 1960s to attract disaffected Jewish youth among the flower children in San Francisco. He founded a synagogue named "The House of Love and Prayer." What was the name of the rabbi?

4-33 During the last 30 years, various groups within the Orthodox community have mounted a large effort to bring secular Jews back to traditional observance. Why was this activity considered necessary?

4-34 The phenomenon of Hasidism was initially popularized for general audiences in the early 20th century by a German-Jewish philosopher in his book *Tales of the Hasidim.* Who was this philosopher, and why was he interested in Hasidism?

4-35 Given its strict levels of observance and old-fashioned dress, why was Hasidism surprisingly successful in transplanting itself to America after World War II?

◀ Appointed by Woodrow Wilson in 1916, Louis D. Brandeis was the first Jewish Supreme Court Justice. During his 23 years serving on the Supreme Court, Brandeis was known as a liberal dissenter, often disagreeing with the conservative majority. He was one of the few supporters of Franklin Delano Roosevelt's New Deal in the early 1930s.

CHAPTER

5

SOCIAL LIFE AND INSTITUTIONS

Ethnic Neighborhoods and Community Life

5-1 Jewish Americans are among the most well-organized ethnic or religious groups in the United States. During the past 150 years, they have established more organizations, institutions, and philanthropic foundations than any other group in the country in spite of their modest size. What reasons might account for this?

5-2 Which Jewish subgroup provided major community leadership from the middle of the 1800s until the 1930s?

5-3 What characterized the attitudes of the German Jews toward the Eastern European Jewish immigrants who followed them?

5-4 As Eastern European Jews took over the leadership of community life beginning in the 1930s, what changes did they bring to leading Jewish organizations and movements?

5-5 The Hebrew Immigration Aid Society (HIAS) was established in 1902. What was the main purpose for its creation?

5-6 Other sources of aid to immigrants were immigrant societies known as Landsmanschaften. Each city or shtetl in Eastern Europe had a society run by some of its emigres. They were probably the single most important social institution for the immigrants. Explain why.

5-7 For many years one of the most important Jewish organizations was the Anti-Defamation League (ADL) of B'nai B'rith. Why was this organization so important?

5-8 From the beginnings of large-scale immigration to America until today, Jews have concentrated in specific urban neighborhoods and suburban towns. What buildings would one expect to see in a community with a large Jewish population?

5-9 Jewish communities, in America and elsewhere, have at times been disrupted by infighting and ideological quarrels. What are some of the issues that have caused conflict in the American Jewish community?

Educational, Cultural, and Community Institutions

5-10 Where was the first synagogue established in the United States, and by whom?

5-11 In most major American cities in the early 20th century, Jewish philanthropists established private hospitals. Why was this done?

5-12 After World War II, the first nonsectarian liberal arts university under Jewish supervision was established in the Boston area. What was the name of the university, and why was it established?

5-13 There are two other liberal arts universities under Jewish supervision in America. Both of them are in New York. What are their names?

5-14 The Simon Wiesenthal Center in Los Angeles was named after the man who devoted his life to hunting down the Nazi officials who were responsible for the Holocaust. What is its purpose?

5-15 The slaughter of European Jews (the Holocaust) in World War II was a subject largely ignored by the organized Jewish community until the 1960s. Why was this so?

5-16 An outpouring of books and films on the subject of the Holocaust has occurred in the last 30 years. This focus on the Holocaust has resulted in the establishment of numerous Holocaust centers, memorials, and museums all over the United States. Where is the largest and most important one located?

5-17 Through the 1960s, Jewish religious and cultural education consisted mainly of afternoon Hebrew schools rather than a parochial school system like the Catholics had built. Were these schools considered successful?

5-18 What type of schools are progressively replacing the afternoon Hebrew school as the main provider of Jewish education?

5-19 What characteristic of Hebrew day schools makes them unusual in American education today?

5-20 A library in Amherst, Massachusetts, houses the largest Yiddish language collection in the world. Why is so much effort and money being invested into preserving books written in a language that is not used by many people?

The Influence of Israel and Zionism

5-21 Theodore Herzl officially launched the Zionist movement from Basel, Switzerland, in 1898. Zionists were committed to forming a Jewish nation. The movement immediately attracted support among the downtrodden Jews of Eastern Europe, some of whom had supported similar ideas that were developing in Russia. Most American Jews, however, were either opposed to Zionism or indifferent to it during its early years (1880–1930). Why was this so?

5-22 Who was one of the first prominent American Jews to become an open supporter of the Zionist movement?

5-23 After World War I and the issuance of the Balfour Declaration, support for the Zionist cause began to grow among American Jews. What events provide evidence of this?

5-24 Even as the Zionist movement began to attract grassroots support among Jewish Americans in the early 20th century, it still was downplayed by much of the community leadership. What was the reason for this?

5-25 In 1928, an organization called the Jewish Agency for Israel was created by American and European Zionists. Its goal was to help fund and build a Jewish national home in Israel. What other purpose did it serve?

5-26 When and why did Zionism finally capture the support of a large majority of America's Jews?

5-27 From the time Israel was established in 1948 until the early 1990s, the American Jewish community organized itself in part to serve as a fundraising apparatus for institutions and causes in Israel. Why has fundraising for Israel played such a central role in Jewish community life?

5-28 In addition to raising money directly for Israel, politically minded Jews established a pro-Israel lobby in Washington, D.C., in the 1950s called the American Israel Public Affairs Committee (AIPAC). How has AIPAC stood out from other lobbies in the political life of Washington?

Recent Trends

5-29 After World War II, many American Jews moved to the suburbs. How was community life maintained once Jews were no longer living in small homogenous neighborhoods?

5-30 The late Rabbi Meir Kahane founded the Jewish Defense League in 1968 in Brooklyn, New York. What was the original purpose of his movement?

5-31 The current rate of intermarriage between Jews and gentiles is between 40 and 50 percent. How is this affecting the nature of Jewish family life?

5-32 What impact does intermarriage have on the future of the Jewish community?

◀ Anne Frank, a young Jewish girl, hid with her family in a secret attic apartment in Amsterdam for two years before they were discovered by the Nazis. She kept a diary of the events of her life during the Holocaust. *The Diary of Anne Frank* is not only one of the most well-known books today, but also one of the most poignant accounts of the horrific events that all but wiped out the European Jewish population during World War II. Anne Frank died in a German concentration camp in 1945.

GROUP CHARACTERISTICS

Demographic Data and Characteristics

6-1 Approximately how many Jews live in the United States, and what percent of the total population are they?

6-2 What state is and has been the center of the Jewish population in America since the 19th century?

6-3 Approximately what percent of the Jewish population of America is of Ashkenazi (European) origin?

6-4 Is there a characteristic Jewish physical appearance?

6-5 In spite of their poverty, many Jewish male immigrants were literate when they first came to America. This culture of literacy and respect for learning produced in later generations the best-educated ethnic group in the United States. In the 1980s, approximately what percent of Jewish adults born in the U.S. were college graduates?

6-6 One of the stereotypical Jewish characters is the Jewish mother. She has been portrayed sympathetically and lovingly in a famous Yiddish song from the vaudeville era, "My Yiddische Mama." She has also been portrayed more scathingly by people such as Woody Allen. How do these portraits differ?

6-7 The Jewish culture from Eastern Europe stressed the importance of being verbal and expressive. In contemporary American society this attribute has resulted in a disproportionate role for Jews in the field of psychotherapy—both as therapists and patients. What four Jewish women have established national followings as advice-givers for people with interpersonal problems?

Cuisine

6-8 Over the last five years, the kosher food industry in America has been growing at the rate of 10 to 12 percent per year. It is one of the fastest growing segments of the food industry. What accounts for this growth?

6-9 What are some of the best-known foods associated with European Jewish cuisine?

6-10 The once stereotypical image of Jewish food was the old-style kosher delicatessen. An order of overflowing hot pastrami on rye with potato chips and a pickle was typical fare years ago. Why have these delis nearly disappeared in the last 30 years, and what type of kosher restaurants have taken their place?

Sectarian Groups

6-11 What are the names of the largest Hasidic groups in the United States today, and where were they originally from?

6-12 There are 40 Hasidic sects in America today. The best-known among them is a group whose chief rabbi, Menachem Mendel Schneerson, died several years ago. This group is known for its outreach activities, its prominence in the media, and conflicts that have emerged with its African-American neighbors in Crown Heights, Brooklyn. What is the name of this Hasidic group?

6-13 The Satmar Hasidim, based in Brooklyn and originally from Hungary, are the largest of the Hasidic groups. Why are they considered unusual even by other Hasidim?

6-14 One of the most renowned Hasidic rebbes from the 18th century was Rabbi Nachman of Bratzslav. The Bratzslaver Hasidim exist today in New York and Israel. What peculiar characteristic distinguishes them?

6-15 Of the many Hasidic groups in America, all but one take their name from the small towns in Eastern Europe from which they came before World War II. What is the one exception?

Recent Trends

6-16 For the last 150 years, the Jewish population has been disproportionately active in political and social causes—both within its own community and in the broader society. This activity has mainly been guided by a secular, liberal approach to social issues. How has this approach begun to change in the last 20 years?

6-17 At one time, the main division in the American Jewish community was between Sephardic and Ashkenazic Jews. Later it was between the German and the Eastern European Jews. What is the main division today?

6-18 In Europe and America, some Jews in the past chose to convert to Christianity in order to gain social acceptance or gain access to political and professional opportunities that would otherwise be closed to them. Why is this no longer necessary in America?

6-19 The number of Jews who convert to Christianity in America is about equal to the number of gentiles who convert to Judaism. (Neither number is large). What does this reflect about American society?

6-20 Since 1948, between 80,000 and 100,000 American Jews have moved to Israel. What impact has this had on Israel and the Jewish community in America?

Jewish Wedding Traditions

Because the Jewish marriage ceremony establishes a new family within the community, tradition plays a large part in wedding celebrations. Wedding rituals vary widely within individual sects of Judaism and among individuals, but a few traditions are common to all. Marriage is called *kiddushin* within traditional literature, a term that translates as "dedication" or "sanctification," emphasizing the spiritual bond between the couple to be married. The marriage ceremony revolves around this double emphasis—the family's place within both a social heritage and a spiritual one.

A *ketuvah*, or marriage contract, is drawn up at some time before the ceremony, occasionally at an engagement reception called a *vort*. The beginning of the ceremony is known as the *chuppah*, or "canopy." The chuppah is held over the couple, usually outside under the stars, as a symbol of God's blessing to Abraham that his people would be "as the stars of the heavens." After the ring is given to the bride, the *sheva brachos*, or seven blessings, are recited over a full cup of wine. This part of the ceremony may include a prayer that the Temple in Jerusalem will be rebuilt, or the groom may step on a wine glass, breaking it. These customs serve as reminders of Israel's history even in the time of greatest joy. The ceremony is followed with a festive meal to welcome the couple into the community.

▲ Clarinetist Benny Goodman was one of the great musicians and band leaders of the "swing era" of the 1930s and 1940s. Goodman faced discrimination as a Jew but hired members of another minority group, African Americans, as musicians for his small ensembles, where some of his best work was produced. He helped start the careers of many great musicians and vocalists, including legendary singer Billie Holiday.

CHAPTER

7

CULTURAL LIFE

Yiddish Culture

7-1 Yiddish is the most widely spoken language the Jews have ever used. Where did it come from?

7-2 Why was the Yiddish language so beloved by the Jews who spoke it, in spite of its hodge-podge character?

7-3 Abraham Cahan was one of the most important figures for the Yiddish-speaking Jewish immigrants who came to America from Eastern Europe. Why was he so important?

7-4 The best-known contributor to *The Forward* was a man who wrote stories in his native Yiddish. His work was later translated into all the major languages of the world, and he won the Nobel Prize for Literature in 1978. What is his name?

7-5 The works of the writer mentioned in the previous question dealt mostly with secular subjects, including love and relationships with women. This would have displeased his father. Why?

7-6 In the late 19th and early 20th centuries, what was the most popular subject of the Yiddish poets and writers who came from Eastern Europe to New York?

7-7 Fiction in the Yiddish language flourished in America possibly more than it did in Eastern Europe from 1900 to the 1930s. Who were the most distinguished Yiddish writers during this period?

7-8 Sholom Aleichem, the most distinguished and popular of all Yiddish writers, immigrated from Russia to America in 1914 and died a few years later. One hundred thousand mourners attended his funeral. What is his best-known work?

7-9 The era of the Yiddish theater began in Eastern Europe in the 1870s and quickly spread to immigrant communities in America. Certain sectors of the Jewish community in both Europe and America strongly opposed it. Where did this opposition come from?

7-10 One of the most beloved Yiddish folk songs about raisins and almonds got its start in the Yiddish theater. What is the name of this song in Yiddish?

7-11 In the first few decades of the 20th century, people attempted to establish bilingual Yiddish/English parochial schools. They thought this would promote the growth of a secular Jewish culture in America. Why did this effort fail?

7-12 How was Yiddish preserved as a living language in America?

7-13 What are some common Yiddish words used in colloquial American English?

Music

7-14 What Jewish American songwriter wrote the popular tunes "White Christmas" and "God Bless America"?

7-15 Who were some of the Jewish-American performers from immigrant backgrounds who popularized a type of music-hall entertainment called vaudeville that was popular between 1880 and 1930? (They later appeared on television comedy shows.)

7-16 Tin Pan Alley in New York City produced some of America's most beloved songwriters and songs before World War II. One of its most famous products, George Gershwin, is best known for an opera he wrote in 1935 depicting the struggling lives of poor southern blacks. What was the name of this opera?

7-17 George Gershwin helped create and popularize an American form of music that was a combination of classical and jazz music. Name one of his most acclaimed pieces.

7-18 Benny Goodman was a talented clarinetist, but his greatest accomplishment was as a band leader. What is he best known for?

7-19 What social achievement is credited to Benny Goodman?

7-20 American musical theater, both on Broadway and in Hollywood, was largely invented by Jews. Who were the two great creative duos of the Broadway musical after World War II?

7-21 What are the names of some famous Rodgers and Hammerstein Broadway musicals?

7-22 What are the names of some famous Lerner and Loewe musicals?

7-23 Stephen Sondheim, another great Broadway composer and lyricist, was unique in that he wrote both the music and lyrics for most of his works. Name some of his shows.

7-24 One of the most important folk/rock artists of the 1960s was a young Jewish man from Minnesota. What is his name, and what did he contribute to popular music?

7-25 After World War I, many American symphony orchestras reached the level of the best orchestras in Europe. This was partly due to an influx of European-trained conductors of mostly Jewish background. These men led a number of important orchestras. Who were the conductors, and which cities' orchestras did they lead?

7-26 Who was the first American-born conductor of Jewish origin to lead a major symphony?

7-27 Many of the world's leading violinists during the last 50 years were of Jewish background. Who are they?

7-28 America has produced only a handful of world-class composers of classical music. One of them was the Brooklyn-born son of Jewish immigrants. He wrote music in many different styles and genres (such as neoclassical, folk, and jazz) and is most famous for his compositions *Appalachian Spring* and *Fanfare for the Common Man*. Who was he?

7-29 Of the many famous Jewish opera singers, two were first trained as cantors (chanters of prayers in a synagogue). Who were they?

7-30 In the last 20 years, a type of Jewish music that originated in Eastern Europe has experienced a major revival. What is the name of this music, and what characterizes it?

7-31 What are the usual instruments in a band that plays this type of music?

Comedy

7-32 In the 1950s, Catskill Mountain resorts played host to a collection of Jewish comedians, some of whom later went on to national fame on television, in the movies, or on the nightclub circuit. These comics engaged in a style of humor—a combination of slapstick, self-deprecation, mockery of others and themselves, and irony—that became renowned. What was the name given to this type of humor?

7-33 Who were some of the well-known comedians who got their start playing to Jewish audiences in the Catskills?

7-34 Jewish humor is often distinguished by a biting, sarcastic quality. What other quality does one find in the following translations from Yiddish of humorous curses? "May you win a lottery, and spend it all on doctors." "May you grow so rich your widow's second husband never has to worry about making a living."

Writers

7-35 In the 1920s, a number of prominent American writers settled in Paris and established a literary community. The most famous among them was probably Ernest Hemingway. The most colorful personality in the group, however, was from a Jewish background. Can you name this writer?

7-36 *Call It Sleep* was a novel about Jewish immigrant life that was published in 1934 and received little attention. It was reissued in 1964 and was immediately recognized as a classic. Who was the author of this novel, and why was it unique?

7-37 What was unusual about this author's career?

7-38 *The Children's Hour* and *Little Foxes* were plays written by one of America's foremost playwrights in the 1930s through the 1950s. This woman also wrote the popular short story (and later movie) "Julia." What was her name?

7-39 A slew of Jewish writers rose to prominence in the 1950s for books that drew on their Jewish upbringing in urban neighborhoods and later immersion into the cosmopolitan society of America. Who were some of these writers?

7-40 Chaim Potok was ordained a Conservative rabbi but achieved recognition as a writer. He wrote a series of novels about the Hasidic and Orthodox community in Brooklyn after World War II. What are the names of some of his books?

7-41 The author of numerous books including *The Messiah of Stockholm* and *The Shawl* is one of the few contemporary Jewish writers who is religiously observant. What is her name?

Intellectual Life

7-42 Which university in New York was known in the mid–20th century as the poor man's Harvard?

7-43 American intellectual life from the 1940s until the late 20th century centered largely in New York City. A group of writers, social critics, and commentators known as the "New York Intellectuals" were the acknowledged leaders of this intellectual elite. What influential journals did they publish?

7-44 A preeminent literary critic of his generation also wrote autobiographical accounts of his generation of Jewish intellectuals from New York. What is his name?

7-45 The radical intellectuals of the New Left combined with pop culture figures to produce an American counterculture in the 1960s. Many of the leading figures in this counterculture were Jews. A particularly well-known member of this so-called beat generation—a poet and writer—died in New York in 1997. What was his name, and what was he known for?

7-46 Commemorating the Holocaust became a major concern in Jewish cultural life starting in the 1960s after the publication of two important accounts of the subject. What were the names of these two books?

7-47 Throughout this century, Jews have frequently been the leading ideologues of left wing and liberal political movements. Recently there has been a trend in the opposite direction. Some of the leading advocates of conservative political and social positions today are Jews. Why has this shift occurred?

Films

7-48 The first feature-length talking film produced in American film history came out in 1927. What was the name of this film, and who was the leading actor?

7-49 Until the 1960s, Hollywood executives were afraid to produce movies that had ethnic characters and themes unless they were stock caricatures. They feared the general public would consider these films parochial and uninteresting or offensive. The great box office success in 1960 of the film version of a Leon Uris novel convinced them that movies with Jewish or Israeli themes could sell. Since then many have been produced. What is the name of the Uris novel, and what is it about?

7-50 In the 1970s, Israeli actor Chaim Topol starred in the movie version of a Broadway hit about the inhabitants of a small Jewish town in Eastern Europe and their travails. What was the name of this movie and play?

7-51 Contemporary Jewish-American film maker Steven Spielberg has created popular entertainment films known for their fantasy and special effects as well as serious films about oppression and racism. Can you name some films in each category?

7-52 Woody Allen is known as an American film writer and director who makes films as a form of artistic expression with a specific view of life. His movies are generally stories about angst-ridden characters pursuing life and love in a comically inept manner. Name some of his most acclaimed movies.

Klezmer Music

Traditional forms of Jewish music have had a profound influence on several new 20th century forms of music in America. Klezmer in particular has been recognized as a major influence on early jazz and swing. Klezmer began as a popular form of music in Eastern Europe as early as the 18th century, when traveling musicians known as *klezmorim* would travel from town to town. It incorporates many different elements, drawing largely from the Yiddish folk song; klezmer means "tool of song" in Hebrew. The violin and clarinet are popular instruments for klezmer. With its driving beat, klezmer is heavily participatory, great music for dancing and festivals.

Although the musical tradition was nearly eradicated during the days of the Nazi regime, klezmer music is currently enjoying a revival. The roots of klezmer originate from many different musical sources and traditions, and today it is often infused with elements of rock and jazz. Klezmer thrives on a diversity of influences and continues to entertain all kinds of audiences.

▲ In the 1930s, African Americans and Jewish Americans became political allies. Both groups were subject to discrimination and found greater strength by working together rather than alone. Jews helped found the National Association for the Advancement of Colored People, or NAACP, which still exists today. But since the 1960s, the differences between the two groups have caused them to go their separate ways and support different causes.

CHAPTER

8

POLITICAL PARTICIPATION

Ideological Approaches

8-1 In the late 19th century many ideological and social movements grew up among the Jews of Eastern Europe. These movements were later brought to America. Name some of these movements.

8-2 Which two elements of the American Constitution were most appreciated by European Jewish immigrants?

8-3 American Jews have always had a high rate of voter participation. What are some of the reasons for this?

8-4 Some ethnic groups in America have used politics as a way to advance their status and reap economic rewards. Other groups have focused on economic success first and gone into politics later. Into which category do the Jews fit?

8-5 In the 1920s, American Jews became strong supporters of the Democratic Party at the national level. Why was this so?

8-6 During the Depression years, the Communist and Socialist Parties in America gained popularity. Most of the people who voted for these parties were non-Jews, but a disproportionate share of the leadership of the Communist Party were Jews. Why were so many Jewish immigrants from Russia and their American-born children initially attracted to communist ideology?

8-7 After Stalin's crimes and the economic failures of communism had been publicized, leftist causes still claimed the loyalty of many Jews right up to the 1960s. This was true even though Jews in America were experiencing a universal rise in economic status. How can this be explained?

8-8 During the years when large eastern and midwestern cities were dominated by Irish-run political machines, Jewish activists often belonged to the opposition. What political role did they play?

World War II and the Holocaust

8-9 During the Great Depression (in the 1930s), anti-Semitism in America increased. What radio personality was responsible for delivering anti-Semitic diatribes in his weekly programs?

8-10 The rise of Nazism in Germany during the 1930s encouraged Nazi sympathizers in America to become more outspoken in their distaste for Jews and in their sympathy for the policies of Hitler's Germany. What prominent American public figures were among these Nazi sympathizers?

8-11 The Jewish community strongly supported Franklin D. Roosevelt when he became president, in spite of the fact that he did not allow Jewish refugees trying to escape the Holocaust to enter the United States. How can this be explained?

8-12 How has awareness of the Holocaust had an impact on American policy toward Israel since its establishment in 1948?

Politics and the State of Israel

8-13 President Truman was the first head of state to grant political recognition to Israel after it was established in 1948. Truman's State Department and other advisors had a more negative view of Israel's creation. What was it that swayed the president in favor of recognizing Israel immediately?

8-14 Why was the Six Day War a turning point in relations between American Jews and Israel?

8-15 The Six Day War was also viewed in a religious manner by many Orthodox Jews. They saw the capture of the biblical lands of Judea and Samaria as a fulfillment of biblical prophecies about the return of the Jewish people to Jerusalem and the rest of the land of Israel. What impact did the events of the war have on Jewish religious life throughout the world?

8-16 Right after the Israeli victory in the Six Day War, a cocktail party was held at the house of Hollywood movie producer Jack Warner. He raised $2.5 million in one hour to aid Israel (in today's money that would be about $10 million). The largest donor was composer and trumpeter Herb Alpert. What was the significance of this event?

8-17 After the Six Day War, with encouragement from official Jewish organizations, the United States became the main benefactor and supporter of Israel in international politics. This eventually led to American involvement in the Arab-Israeli peace process, culminating in the Camp David accords of 1979. Who were the three political leaders who participated in drawing up these accords?

8-18 During President Reagan's two terms in office, Israel was made a strategic partner of the United States in the Cold War and participated in the Star Wars Missile Defense Programs. What changes occurred in Israeli and American Jewish life during the 1980s that encouraged President Reagan to align with Israel?

8-19 During the 1980s, the United States government gave three billion dollars a year to Israel in foreign aid. What was the other major source of financial aid that went to Israel?

8-20 The Oslo Peace Accords were signed in 1993 by the Palestine Liberation Organization (PLO), led by Yassir Arafat, and the Israeli government, led by Yitzhak Rabin and Shimon Peres. Where was the ceremony held to celebrate these accords?

Contemporary Politics and Issues

8-21 Jewish and African Americans were political allies from the 1930s, when Jews helped found the NAACP, to the 1960s civil rights movement. In recent decades the relationship between the two groups has deteriorated, and they are no longer political allies. What are some reasons for this?

8-22 Why did the Jewish community, which initially supported affirmative action for African Americans and other non-white minorities, eventually become critical of it?

8-23 The activists of the New Left in the 1960s were dispropor-tionately Jewish. Who were the founders and most flamboyant members of the Yippie movement? What happened to them in later decades?

8-24 Some of the most important academic leaders of the New Left were Jewish professors at universities in the Boston area. Who were some of these professors, and what were they opposed to?

8-25 By the 1980s, a group of liberals who were dissatisfied with the condition of American liberalism advocated new policies. Calling themselves "neo-conservatives," they became an important influence on U.S. public policy. Many of the founders of the neo-conservatism movement were Jews. Why did they become critical of American liberalism?

8-26 The decline of the liberal ideological outlook among the Jewish population was most vividly demonstrated by the 1997 New York mayoral election. What was the outcome in that election?

8-27 The first Jewish representatives in Congress from the early 20th century generally came from districts in large cities (mainly New York) where their were large numbers of Jews. How has the situation changed today?

◀ Emma Goldman was one of the early feminists and a leader of the No Conscription League in New York. Proponents of anarchy, the abolition of laws and government, she and Alexander Berkman were convicted of conspiracy against the draft law during World War I, sentenced to two years in jail, and fined $10,000 each.

CHAPTER

9

IMPORTANT PERSONALITIES and PEOPLE OF ACCOMPLISHMENT

Intellectuals and Cultural Figures

9-1 In 1942 the United States government started the Manhattan Project. Its goal was to build the first atom bomb. Most of the top scientists who worked on this project were European Jewish refugees or American Jews. Who was the Jewish-American physicist who directed this project?

9-2 Psychoanalysis was introduced to America by Jewish refugees from Germany and Austria. What German Jew was the best-known psychoanalyst in America during the 1930s and 1940s?

9-3 The first Jewish journalist to achieve great acclaim in high political circles started his career by writing biting editorials and columns in Pulitzer's *World,* then the *New York Herald Tribune,* and finally the *Washington Post.* His career stretched from 1918 to his retirement in 1967. Who was he?

9-4 Who was the first Jew to be appointed a Supreme Court justice?

9-5 A famous writer on the Holocaust, Elie Wiesel, came from a Hasidic family in Romania. Which Hasidic group was his family associated with?

9-6 Abraham Flexner made an extremely important contribution to medical education in America. What did he do?

9-7 What is Edward Teller known for?

9-8 Although art was an unknown craft in the Jewish world of Eastern Europe (due to a religious rule against making graven images), in America many Jews became prominent artists. Name several of the most famous artists who came from a Jewish background.

Political Leaders and Public Figures

9-9 What Jewish immigrant of the late 18th century helped finance the American Revolution?

9-10 Jews have played a prominent role in the politics of both New York City and New York state during most of the 20th century. Who was the first Jewish governor of New York?

9-11 One of New York City's most beloved mayors was Fiorello LaGuardia. He appealed to a wide cross-section of New York's ethnic groups during his terms in office (1934–45). What about his family background contributed to his appeal?

9-12 The first Jewish mayor of New York was Abraham Beame. He was elected in 1973. The second Jewish mayor was more colorful and outspoken and became a national personality during his three terms in office. Who was he?

9-13 What man with Jewish roots ran for president on the Republican Party ticket?

9-14 President Nixon appointed the first Jewish secretary of state in 1973. Henry Kissinger is remembered largely for three accomplishments. What were these?

9-15 Another secretary of state, Madeleine Albright, was raised a Catholic and converted to the Episcopal Church when she married. Why is she considered Jewish by origin?

Entertainment and Sports

9-16 Barbara Streisand is considered one of the most talented women in the entertainment industry. During her career she has excelled in what area of entertainment?

9-17 Who were some of the best known Jewish baseball players who reached All-Star status?

9-18 For what incident that took place during the 1965 World Series is Sandy Koufax, a Brooklyn Dodger pitcher, known?

9-19 What Jewish American won the most Olympic Gold Medals for an individual in one Olympics?

9-20 While there have never been many Jewish professional basketball players, the former coach and general manager of the most successful NBA team ever is Jewish. Who is he, and what was his team?

Military Service

9-21 Several people from the small number of Jews living in the United States during the late 18th and early 19th centuries distinguished themselves militarily. What person was the most prominent of these?

9-22 Who was the first Jewish admiral of the United States Navy?

9-23 What American of German-Jewish origin composed the famous poem on the Statue of Liberty?

9-24 What Jewish immigrant from Russia became one of the leading proponents of anarchism and was an early advocate of feminist ideas?

9-25 Who was the first president of the American Federation of Labor (AFL), and why were his views noteworthy?

9-26 The only woman prime minister of Israel was originally an American citizen. Who was she, and where was she from?

9-27 For what crime has Jonathan Pollard, an American Jew, been sentenced to life in prison?

Jewish Community Organizations

The American Jewish community has often struggled to uphold and defend a sense of group identity. One outlet developed over the years—the neighborhood organization—has been instrumental in maintaining the community. In the first half of this century, groups like the American Jewish Conference and the American Jewish Congress led community organizations to their place of prominence within Jewish-American life. Currently, the largest network of Jewish community organizations in both the United States and the world is B'nai B'rith. B'nai B'rith provides support for its members while encouraging activism within the Jewish community. Its services range from selling insurance to its members to providing family counseling and promoting Jewish life on college campuses.

Perhaps the most important branch of B'nai B'rith is the Anti-Defamation League (ADL), its political action group. The Anti-Defamation League was founded in the United States in 1913 as the first organization of its kind to fight anti-Semitism. Among its many functions, the ADL serves as an information source on all forms of organized bigotry. Its annual Audit of Anti-Semitic Incidents does national polling to keep watch on bias crimes against Jewish-Americans. Both B'nai B'rith and the ADL are leaders in the effort to preserve a strong sense of Jewish fellowship in America.

Answers

◀ It is common, especially among Ashkenazi Jews, for the books of the Torah to be preserved on scrolls, as they were thousands of years ago.

1 ORIGINS

Antiquity

1-1   Abraham is considered the first Jew. He traveled to ancient Israel (or the land of Canaan, as it was first called in the Bible) around 1800 B.C. According to the Bible, God told Abraham to go there from his home in Mesopotamia.

1-2   Abraham; his son, Isaac; and his grandson Jacob are the Patriarchs.

1-3   The Matriarchs include Sarah, the wife of Abraham; Rebecca, the wife of Isaac; and Rachel and Leah, the wives of Jacob.

1-4   They settled in Israel between 1800 and 1700 B.C. Their descendants migrated to Egypt to escape a famine. While in Egypt, they were enslaved by the Pharaohs.

1-5   They returned when Moses led them out of Egypt after 400 years of slavery (around 1200 B.C.).

1-6   After the exodus from Egypt, the Israelites passed through the Sinai Desert where, according to tradition, they received the Torah (Jewish Scriptures) from God on Mount Sinai.

1-7   There are many interpretations of current archeological evidence. Some experts believe the evidence supports the

story of the Israelites conquering Canaan by force.
Other authorities believe the evidence suggests many
Canaanites became Israelites by choice. They were grad-
ually absorbed into the Israelite culture.

1-8   Other faiths that grew out of Judaism include Christianity,
Islam, and many small offshoots of both these major
religions.

1-9   The kingdom of King David (1000-960 B.C.) included
part of present-day Lebanon, Syria, Jordan, Egypt, and
the disputed territories of the West Bank and Gaza Strip.

1-10   Most of the Jews then living in Israel went into exile in
Babylon. This was the beginning of the Diaspora (the
dispersion of Jews outside of Israel). The term Diaspora
is also used to refer to the Jews living outside of Israel as
well as to the land outside Palestine in which they lived.

1-11   The Persian Empire, led by Cyrus, conquered the Babylonians and took control of all their territorial possessions.
The Persians allowed the Jewish community in Israel to
be rebuilt.

1-12   The Jewish exiles built the Second Temple in 516 B.C.

1-13   Since the Babylonian Exile (about 2,500 years ago), Jews
have looked to Israel as their religious center.

1-14   The community in Egypt, which was centered in Alexan-
dria, and the community in Babylonia were the most
important Jewish communities outside Israel.

1-15   The Romans conquered Judea (Israel) and forcibly killed,
subjugated, or encouraged the emigration of most of the
Jews under their control. They also destroyed the Second
Temple in Jerusalem in A.D. 70.

1-16 A code of Jewish Law—the Talmud—helped standardize religious practice, while the continuous study of the Torah (Jewish Scriptures) created a common focus for community life.

1-17 Iraq (Babylon), Iran (Persia), Ethiopia, and Yemen had Jewish communities as early as 1000 B.C. The Jewish community of southern India probably dates back 2,000 years.

1-18 The two major groups are the Sephardi (from Spain) and the Ashkenazi (from German-speaking lands of Central Europe).

1-19 During the Middle Ages, Jews in Spain and Central Europe were persecuted for three major reasons: 1) They were caught in the conflicts between Christians and Muslims that led up to and included the Crusades; 2) Probably because of their strict dietary laws and careful hygiene, fewer Jews died of the bubonic plague, and many of their gentile neighbors began to believe the plague was the result of a Jewish plot; and 3) Jewish leaders in Spain supported the losing side during a civil war, so as punishment Spanish Jews were forced to convert to Christianity or flee the country. Many Jews fled to Poland. By the 15th century, Poland had a very progressive monarchy that welcomed the Jews for economic reasons and gave them physical and political protection.

1-20 Jews were an important part of the economy, serving as moneylenders, merchants, physicians, and translators.

1-21 Moses Maimonides (1135-1204) was a rabbi, theologian, philosopher, and physician who made important contributions in all those areas.

1-22 The Jewish communities in Islamic countries had a recognized and protected legal status. Forced conversion was rare, and mass slaughter was generally discouraged if not forbidden for religious reasons. Their condition, therefore, was infinitely better than that of Jews in Europe. However, they had inferior political status to

▼ A page from Moses Maimonides's Mishne Torah, a religious code drafted in 1180. Initially met with opposition, the Mishne Torah is now accepted as an authoritative code of Jewish law and has been translated into many languages. Maimonides is one of the most revered Jewish philosophers.

Muslims and suffered various forms of economic and
social discrimination.

Modern Europe

1-23 The pope ordered that all Jews be segregated in their own
neighborhoods. They were not allowed to go out at
night and were kept from all but the lowliest jobs. They
were also forced to wear yellow hats as a sign that they
were Jewish. The areas in which Jews were confined in
Italy were called ghettoes. Because of this Papal edict,
the idea of isolating Jews and discriminating against
them spread throughout Europe.

1-24 Baruch Spinoza's ideas were considered so heretical that in
1656 he was excommunicated from the Jewish community in Amsterdam where he lived. This was particularly
significant because the Jewish community in Amsterdam
was known for its respect of diversity and dissent.

1-25 Israel Baal Shem Tov emphasized the importance of the
emotional and spiritual aspects of religious devotion
rather than the scholarly aspects that traditionally had
been stressed in Eastern Europe.

1-26 Jews were allowed to live only in a restricted region of the
empire known as the Pale of Settlement. This area
consisted of what is today Central and Eastern Poland,
Western Ukraine, the Baltic States, and Belarus.

1-27 Benjamin Disraeli.

1-28 From 1850 to 1945, nationalist and racist movements in
Europe grew in size and influence, culminating in
Nazism, which glorified ethnic and racial purity. The
Jews were seen by the followers of all these movements
as unwanted outsiders.

1-29 The Jewish population exploded during the 19th century for several reasons: Jewish families had a high birth rate; there were few massacres of Jews, as there had been in earlier centuries; the Jewish population was not affected by serious disease epidemics; and there was a low rate of conversion to other religions.

1-30 They emigrated in huge numbers to Central and Western Europe and to the Americas. They also supported radical and revolutionary political movements in Europe.

1-31 The rabbi symbolized the importance of the religious way of life in the shtetl. The matchmaker was a symbol of the importance attached to marriage and family life. The beggar symbolized the importance of giving to the poor in a traditional Jewish community.

1-32 Jews emigrated to the United States (roughly two-thirds of the total number), Argentina, Brazil, England, France, Germany, Austria, South Africa, and Palestine.

1-33 Jews supported the liberal forces because they advocated individual rights, equal rights for all citizens, a secular state, and general tolerance.

1-34 Jews were often seen by the Muslims as being too pro-Western because they received a Western-style education and they prospered professionally and economically much more than the Muslim majority under colonial rule. They became victims of mob attacks in many Arab countries in the 20th century as the traditional forms of political rule began to crumble. When the state of Israel was established in 1948, most Jews in the Arab world were driven out of these countries. Most of these refugees went to Israel.

1-35 The Bolsheviks and their successor, the Soviet Communist Party, wiped out the religious life of the Jews partly because they were categorically antireligious and did the same thing to other religious groups. However, the communists also went to great pains to eradicate any vestige of Jewish culture due to a particular fear and dislike of the Jews. The Nazis were anti-Semitic because it was part of their ideology of racial purity and Aryan superiority.

1-36   In 1924, the United States Congress passed the Johnson-Reed Bill. It severely restricted the number of immigrants from Southern and Eastern Europe. Those regions were where most Jews in Europe lived.

1-37   The conference was a failure. No country, including the United States, was willing to offer asylum to any significant number of Jewish refugees or to press the Nazis to alter their policies.

1-38   Refugee sites were considered in Angola, Southwest Africa, and Alaska.

1-39   The majority of states in the newly founded United Nations were from Europe or Latin America. These states felt a certain amount of guilt over their complicity in or indifference to the Holocaust.

The Contemporary World

1-40   During the biblical period, the Jews were known as Hebrews, the Children of Israel (Bene Yisrael), or Israelites. In the last 2,000 years they have been referred to as Jews, a term taken from the Latin and Greek words for Judea (the ancient kingdom of Israel). Citizens of modern Israel are called Israelis.

1-41   Before World War II, most of the world's Jewish population was in Eastern or Western Europe or Russia. The dominant language of this population was Yiddish. Today less than 10 percent of Jews live in Europe, and the Jewish population of Russia is disappearing as Jews either emigrate or are absorbed into the larger culture. Most Diaspora Jews today live in English-speaking countries, mainly in America.

1-42 Because of the Holocaust and because of some Jews being absorbed into the larger cultures in which they live, the size of the Diaspora has shrunk during this century. Meanwhile, due to immigration and natural growth, the population of Israel has grown to roughly 35 percent of the total Jewish population. America currently contains about 45 percent of the total population.

1-43 There are three Jewish communities that might compare to the modern Jewish community in the United States: the community of Spain during its golden age (between A.D. 1000 and 1492); the community of ancient Egypt during one of its golden ages (fourth century B.C. through the second century A.D.); and the Babylonian community in its golden age (third century A.D. through the fifth century A.D.).

2 ARRIVAL IN AMERICA

Waves of Immigration

2-1 Eight different waves of Jewish immigrants came to America: Sephardic Jews (1650–1750); German Jews (1830–60); Eastern European Jews, first wave (1870–1924); Eastern European Jews, second wave (1945–50); Israelis (1948–90); Syrian Jews (1948–1960); Russian Jews (1974–present); and Iranian Jews (1979–90).

2-2 Some of these immigrants came directly from Amsterdam, and others came to America from Spain and Portugal via the West Indies or South America.

2-3 They settled mostly in port cities along the East Coast—from Savannah and Charleston in the South, to New York and Newport, Rhode Island, in the North.

2-4 Catholicism was still seen by many American Protestants as a threat. Wars had been waged in Europe between Protestant and Catholic nations. In contrast, it was thought that a relative handful of Jews would not threaten anyone and would bring economic benefits.

2-5 From 1830–60, approximately 150,000 German Jews came to America from Central Europe.

2-6 The German Jews immigrated to America largely looking for economic opportunities and political stability. The

Eastern European Jews came to America mainly to flee persecution, poverty, and wars.

2-7 In Europe, the established churches encouraged anti-Semitism for centuries as part of the broader national culture. As Europe became secularized, this form of hatred took on a racial cast. Anyone who had some Jewish ancestry was considered a Jew. There was also the factor of economic envy. Jews often were merchants in societies made up mostly of peasants. The wealthier Jews

▼ New York's Harlem neighborhood was inhabited by both Jewish immigrants new to America and African Americans in the late 19th century. By 1920, however, the neighborhood was predominantly African American.

became a target for the wrath of the peasants. European governments considered it necessary and desirable to develop cultural unity. The presence of a Jewish minority interfered with this and led to organized attempts by governments to expel, convert, or kill the Jews.

2-8   From the beginning, America had no national church and its people were diverse. American Protestants generally had a much more positive view of the Jews theologically. They associated Jews with the Old Testament, which was an important part of Protestant religious culture. In addition, anti-Semitism in America was never promoted by the government, and mob violence was rare. Anti-Semitism was mostly expressed as genteel snobbery, social exclusion, and quotas. Little of this behavior exists today.

2-9   1) The assassination of Czar Alexander II in 1881 and the official incitement of pogroms (an organized massacre of helpless people); 2) the Kishinev pogrom in 1903; 3) the Bolshevik Revolution; and 4) the Russian Civil War (1918–20).

2-10   Eastern European Jews were attracted by the free, universal public education in America. Such education was not available to them in Czarist Russia, and they saw it as the basis for upward social and economic movement.

2-11   They helped make the American university system the most advanced and accomplished in the world after World War II, an honor that had been held by German universities until then.

2-12   Albert Einstein.

2-13   Syrian Jews come from a community that traces its origins back 2,500 years to the first dispersion after the destruction of the First Temple in Jerusalem. They maintained their close family and community ties after resettling as a group in South Brooklyn in the 1950s. They also sent their children exclusively to religious schools.

2-14 Some citizens left Israel to escape the tension of living in a war zone. Others came for economic and professional advancement.

2-15 Jews were very prominent as members of the intellectual, scientific, and artistic elite of the country. The regime was afraid the nation would suffer if so much talent was allowed to leave the country.

2-16 Soviet Jews come with a very high level of education and professional accomplishment. Also, after 70 years of living under communism, they are not very familiar with traditional Jewish culture—either religious or secular. Many of them are only partly Jewish or are married to non-Jews.

2-17 New Russian immigrants have a strong distaste for left-wing movements and philosophies. They also know very little about how to sustain voluntary community institutions and cultural life, since there was no civil society under communism.

2-18 When the Shah of Iran was overthrown in 1979, the Islamic fundamentalist regime of Ayatollah Khomeini came to power. In response to this, the religious minorities of Iran (Jews, Christians, Bahais) began to leave the country.

Settlement in America

2-19 Washington assured the Jewish community that in America there would be no officially sanctioned religious bigotry against them.

2-20 New York City, the city that contained Ellis Island, was where most Jewish immigrants first stayed in America. About half of them settled there permanently.

2-21 To a group of people used to being a small, insignificant, unappreciated, and usually despised minority, New York was special. It had the largest Jewish population in any city ever in history. It was a city where all aspects of Jewish culture thrived and were visible. It was also the only city in the world, outside of Israel, where political candidates came to get a blessing from a rabbi before election day.

2-22 The neighborhood is Harlem. It was a mixed neighborhood between 1870 and 1920, made up of mostly Jewish and Italian immigrants and of African Americans moving from the South. By the late 1920s, Harlem had become overwhelmingly black, and it remains so.

2-23 Approximately 1,645,000 Jews (28 percent of the total American Jewish population) still live in New York. More than half live in the Northeast. The other large concentrations are in major midwestern cities and the states of California and Florida.

2-24 The first Jews came to Los Angeles at the time of the California Gold Rush in 1849. The real growth of the Jewish population began with the creation of Hollywood in the 1920s.

2-25 These laws encouraged the movement of Jews from urban neighborhoods to suburbia.

2-26 Jews moved to these towns for two main reason: 1) It was necessary to have large numbers of Jews in the same area if they were going to maintain the social ties and environment that sustain a community; 2) Specific towns attracted newly affluent Jews because of their prestige and because of their high quality institutions.

2-27 Such suburbs include Brookline and Newton, Massachusetts (outside Boston); Scarsdale and many other towns in the New York counties of Westchester and Nassau, and the

Connecticut county of Fairfield (outside New York City); Brighton and Pittsford, New York (outside Rochester); Skokie and Evanston, Illinois (outside Chicago).

2-28 Middle-class Cubans exiled from Castro's Cuba and other Hispanics now live in Miami Beach.

2-29 These communities were established by either German or Eastern European Jews who often worked as peddlers or owners of clothing stores. Later generations have gone to college and prefer to work as professionals in urban areas.

3 ECONOMIC LIFE

3-1 1) The diamond industry, which is now dominated by Hasidic Jews; 2) the garment industry, which until 30 years ago was dominated by Jews at all levels; and 3) the film industry in Hollywood, where all but one of the major studios was founded by Jews.

3-2 Jewish Americans achieved a level of upward mobility unmatched by any other immigrant group. By the second generation, most Jews were already in the professional workforce or owners of their own businesses.

3-3 In 1912, he moved to a small town in California called Hollywood and established a movie production company with his brother-in-law that became known as Metro-Goldwyn-Mayer (MGM). He was one of the founders of the motion picture industry in Hollywood.

3-4 It was known for its pioneering role in setting standards for unionized benefits, particularly in the areas of health care, retirement insurance, and educational benefits for its members.

3-5 Many men had traveled to the San Francisco area from 1849 on because of the Gold Rush and other job opportunities in mining. They needed sturdy, ready-to-wear pants for this type of work.

3-6 Shearson Lehman Brothers, Goldman Sachs, and Salomon Brothers.

▲ New York City attracted many of the two million Jewish immigrants that arrived in America between 1881 and 1914. In 1889, the Lower East Side's Hester Street was home to thousands of these newly arrived immigrants.

3-7 Bloomingdales, Sears, Filene's, Abraham and Strauss, and Niemann-Marcus.

3-8 Levitt produced modestly priced suburban housing for returning GIs in a town on Long Island called Levittown.

The community was preplanned, and the builders used prefabricated parts and some assembly-line techniques in construction.

3-9 The Lender family from New Haven, Connecticut, started the mass marketing of Lender's frozen bagels in supermarkets all over America.

3-10 Gambling.

3-11 The Radio Corporation of America (RCA).

3-12 The television set.

3-13 Polaroid.

3-14 Jonas Salk invented the polio vaccine in 1954 using weakened live virus for the vaccine preparation. Subsequently, Albert Sabin invented a vaccine that used dead viruses. The Sabin vaccine is mainly used today.

3-15 Simon and Schuster, Alfred A. Knopf, Viking Press.

3-16 Adolph Ochs bought the *New York Times*. His daughter married Arthur Hays Sulzberger, who became its publisher when his father-in-law died. His grandson is currently its publisher.

3-17 He is known today primarily for Pulitzer Prizes (paid out of money he left in his will), which reward excellence in of journalism, literature, and music.

3-18 Louis D. Brandeis was appointed to the U.S. Supreme Court in 1916 by Woodrow Wilson, and Felix Frankfurter was appointed to the court in 1939 by Franklin D. Roosevelt.

3-19 The United Jewish Appeal (UJA) raises over one billion dollars per year.

3-20 About 30 percent.

3-21 The Jewish religious tradition from which all the immigrants came emphasizes lifelong study as the most honorable pursuit for a young man. Although this tradition referred to the study of the Torah and Talmud and not to secular studies, the value placed on learning can be easily transferred from one subject to another.

4 RELIGIOUS LIFE

Religious Beliefs

4-1 Judaism was the first religion to be monotheistic (one God), unlike other religions of antiquity, which were polytheistic (many gods).

4-2 The covenant was made with the Patriarchs: Abraham, Isaac, and Jacob.

4-3 Judaism includes a belief in the afterlife, but it's not an important part of theology or religious life.

4-4 These were revolutionary ideas compared to the views of other religions of antiquity, which were not at all egalitarian. These ideas were later developed by both Jewish and Christian thinkers and became key elements of Western thought. They contributed to the rise of democratic ideals.

4-5 The narrative accounts in the Torah start at the dawn of creation and cover the historical period from Abraham to the death of Moses.

4-6 1. There is only one God.
2. Do not worship idols.
3. Do not take God's name in vain.
4. Remember the Sabbath and keep it holy.
5. Honor your father and mother.
6. Do not murder.
7. Do not commit adultery.

8. Do not steal.

9. Do not bear false witness against your neighbor.

10. Do not covet your neighbor's property.

4-7 The Messiah is seen as a political leader who will usher in the Messianic Age when he comes. This will be an age of peace and brotherhood and perfection.

4-8 The Talmud is a huge collection of commentaries on the

▼ Holidays such as Rosh Hashanah, Yom Kippur, and Passover are occasions for families to gather together and celebrate their heritage. Symbolic and traditional foods accompany each holiday. The foods eaten during a Passover celebration, such as the one pictured here, commemorate the Israelites' flight from Egypt.

Torah compiled by great rabbis in the third through sixth centuries A.D. in Palestine and Babylonia. It also contains folklore and the religious and civil legal code of Judaism.

4-9 Prophets were individuals who spoke for God. They appeared at critical times to admonish the Israelites to return to God. They outlined the dangers of disobeying God's law. Prophets such as Isaiah developed the idea that when Israel becomes truly loyal to God, the world will experience an age of universal peace.

4-10 Maimonides was a proponent of traditional Judaism, but in his writings he explained Jewish legal concepts using a system of logic drawn from Aristotle. His thinking was written in a clear and logical manner compared to other rabbinic commentators.

4-11 Jerusalem was the capital city of ancient Israel, and it was the place where the holy Temple was built by Solomon. It has remained a center of Jewish pilgrimage and religious life during the thousands of years of the Diaspora.

4-12 According to legend, the star of David is supposed to have originated as a religious symbol in the times of King Solomon or King David. However, its first documented use as a symbol of Judaism and Jewish identity comes from 19th-century Germany. It was adopted by the Zionist movement as a secular symbol for the Jewish people and is still used in that way. It appears on the flag of Israel.

4-13 The engraving is of Roman soldiers carrying off the candelabra after they destroyed the Second Temple and conquered Jerusalem in A.D. 70. It symbolized the destruction of ancient Israel and the subjugation of Jews under Roman rule.

4-14 Two modern holidays are Remembrance Day for the

victims of the Holocaust, and Israeli Independence Day.

4-15 The three holidays are 1) Yom Kippur, the Day of Atonement, during which people ask God to forgive them for the sins they committed in the previous year; 2) Passover, which commemorates the time when the Jewish people were led out of slavery in Egypt by Moses; and 3) Hannukah, which commemorates the rededication of the temple after Judah and the Maccabees retook Jerusalem from the Greeks, who were trying to suppress the Jewish faith.

4-16 People do not work, they attend synagogue, and they eat the Sabbath meal with their family and invited guests.

4-17 Milk and meat products are kept separate, special rules are followed when slaughtering animals, and certain meats (such as pork and shellfish) are never eaten.

4-18 Moses led the Israelites to Mount Sinai, where they received the Torah in a revelation from God. They then spent 40 years wandering through the desert until they reached the land of Caanan.

4-19 During Passover, no products with any leavening agent can be used. This eliminates food such as bread, cookies, and cakes. Also, matzoh and products made out of matzoh meal are the only grain products that can be used.

4-20 The Jews searched the temple in Jerusalem for consecrated oil to light the temple's menorah. They found only one vessel of oil that hadn't been desecrated by the Greeks. It lasted for eight days rather than the expected one day, giving enough time for fresh oil to be prepared.

Customs and Modern Adaptations

4-21 A mezzuzah is a miniature representation of a Torah scroll, and it contains a piece of parchment with a verse from

Deuteronomy (the last book of the five books of Moses).

4-22 The scrolls are placed inside an object known as an ark, which resembles a large closet.

4-23 Most Jewish communities over the past 3,000 years have been located west of Israel. During prayer Jews are supposed to face in the direction of Jerusalem and Israel.

4-24 Boys have a Bar Mitzvah ceremony (Bar Mitzvah means

▼ Mateuz Kos studies for his bar mitzvah and the chance to be seen as an adult in the eyes of the Jewish religion and community. In 1985, Kos became the first Jewish boy in Warsaw, Poland, to be bar mitzvahed after World War II. Reading and understanding portions of the Torah is a large part of the bar mitzvah (bat mitzvah for girls) ceremony.

son of the commandment), and girls have a Bat Mitzvah ceremony (Bat Mitzvah means daughter of the commandment). In Reform communities, these ceremonies usually happen when a person reaches the age of 13, regardless of gender.

4-25 The three major branches of American Judaism are Orthodox, Reform, and Conservative. In general, the following characteristics are true of the three branches of Judaism: 1) Orthodox Jews believe in one God, in living ethical lives by obeying the laws and traditions prescribed in the Torah (Hebrew Bible), and in the special role of the Jewish people in the world; 2) Reform Jews believe in a universal humanism, observe fewer rituals and customs from the Torah, and hold liberal attitudes toward social issues; 3) Conservative Jews hold attitudes and beliefs similar to Reform Jews but observe Jewish rituals and traditions more strictly.

4-26 Traditional Judaism, with its religious laws regulating personal behavior and its emphasis on modesty and family life, finds more in common with conservative social policies and politicians.

4-27 The Reform movement has involved itself greatly in the social and political affairs of the broader society. In the past in Europe or the Islamic world, such involvement would have been unthinkable. The Modern Orthodox have encouraged their members to acquire both a secular and religious education and remain ritually observant while pursuing careers in the professional world, also something unheard of in the past.

Recent Trends

4-28 The Reform branch of Judaism was a strong supporter of Martin Luther King Jr. and the nonviolent phase of the civil rights movement.

4-29 The more liberal branches ordain women as rabbis and allow them to read the Torah publicly in the synagogue. The Orthodox do not allow women such roles.

4-30 These changes have happened as a response to a greater desire among younger Jews for a spiritual life and as a counter to the attraction Orthodox Judaism holds because of its spirituality. Emphasizing tradition may also help prevent some members from losing their Jewish identity and being absorbed into the larger culture.

4-31 The Havurah movement broke down large impersonal suburban synagogues into smaller social units that tailored their activities to the specific interests of each group.

4-32 Rabbi Shlomo Carlebach. Asked why he gave his traditional synagogue such an untraditional name, he replied, "If I called it Temple Israel, no one would come."

4-33 A century ago in Eastern Europe, 95 percent of Jews were Orthodox. By the 1960s in America, the number of Orthodox Jews had decreased to about 5 percent. In order to rejuvenate the Orthodox community, many rabbis felt it was necessary to bring back some of the grandchildren and great-grandchildren of those who had abandoned Orthodoxy.

4-34 The philosopher was Martin Buber. His interest in Hasidism grew out of his studies of human beings' relationships with each other and with God.

4-35 After the war, a number of charismatic Hasidic rebbes were able to attract a small number of Holocaust survivors in Brooklyn and in Israel. They rebuilt their communities by offering leadership and spiritual comfort to people whose lives were shattered by the war.

Their numbers multiplied over two generations because of their large families and because very few members left the communities. In the last 20 years, some of the Hasidic groups have also attracted followers from among Jews who have become disenchanted with the secular lifestyle and culture.

5 SOCIAL LIFE AND INSTITUTIONS

Ethnic Neighborhoods and Community Life

5-1 Over thousands of years, Jews generally lived in their own communities surrounded by hostile or indifferent neighbors. In order to survive, both physically and culturally, they had to provide for their own needs and not rely on the goodwill of others. These habits continue in America.

5-2 Jewish community organizations were led during this period mainly by wealthy progressive-minded German Jews.

5-3 The German Jews generally looked down upon their Eastern European counterparts because they spoke Yiddish (considered a vulgar jargon), were religiously more traditional, and came from the provincial and poverty-stricken shtetls. German Jews were mostly Reform in religious practice and were more cultured and prosperous than the Eastern European immigrants.

5-4 The Reform movement became more deferential to traditional religious practices and introduced some Hebrew into the prayer services. Leading Jewish organizations became supportive of the Zionist movement rather than being hostile to it, as they had been previously.

5-5 HIAS provided economic aid to immigrants on their arrival and helped them adapt to American society. These services are now performed to some degree by government social welfare agencies, but such agencies didn't exist at the time.

5-6 They provided familiar faces and a welcoming social environment for uprooted immigrants coming from small towns to big, impersonal cities. The Landsmanschaften usually built their own synagogues and provided other services. The immigrant Jews remained very attached to and nostalgic about the little towns they had come from in Eastern Europe.

5-7 For centuries, the main preoccupation of Jewish communi-

▼ Immigrants landing on Ellis Island in New York had to pass a series of health inspections and background checks for criminal records before they could enter the country. Because of the large number of immigrants arriving daily during the early 1900s, the wait seemed endless to those who had just made the long journey.

ties was defending themselves against anti-Semitism. The mission of the ADL has been to uncover anti-Semitic groups or institutions and bring the power of the legal system and public opinion against them.

5-8   A Jewish community usually includes several synagogues, a Kosher butcher shop, a Kosher bakery, other Kosher food establishments, and several Hebrew schools.

5-9   In the first half of this century the main disagreements were between the religiously liberal and the traditional; the communists and the socialists; the socialists and the liberal democrats; and the Zionists and the anti-Zionists. Today the main disagreements are between the liberals and the neo-conservatives; the pro-Israeli right and the pro-Israeli left; and the Orthodox and both the Reform and the Conservative.

Educational, Cultural, and Community Institutions

5-10   Touro Synagogue was the first permanent synagogue. It was built in Newport, Rhode Island, in the 1750s. Its most generous benefactors were the Touro family, a Sephardic family that came from the West Indies.

5-11   They wanted to guarantee Jewish patients access to Kosher food and religious services. Also, these hospitals enabled Jewish doctors to rise to prominent positions that they were excluded from in other hospitals because of discrimination.

5-12   Brandeis University was created to be a top institution comparable to the other elite private colleges in the Northeast at a time when those colleges still had quotas for their Jewish applicants to keep the number of Jewish students down.

5-13   Yeshiva University and Touro College.

5-14 The center publicizes issues related to the Holocaust and anti-Semitism.

5-15 In the years after the war (1945–60), American Jews were primarily interested in improving their economic status and in gaining acceptance in American society. They also wanted to help establish and secure the existence of the state of Israel. They were reluctant to emphasize their victimization.

5-16 The largest museum is on the mall in the center of Washington, D.C.

5-17 Generally, the schools weren't successful. They did not instill great religious commitment or cultural knowledge in their graduates. Enrollment in this type of school has gone down by more than half since the 1960s.

5-18 Hebrew day schools (all-day schools) have mushroomed in the last 30 years and are now in every Jewish community of several thousand people. These private schools include both general studies in English and Judaic (mainly religious) studies in Hebrew.

5-19 Like Catholic schools and Christian (Protestant) schools, they provide both secular and religious education. Unlike these schools, however, they provide education in two languages—either English and Hebrew or English and Yiddish. Most other bilingual schools that have existed in America have not survived for very long.

5-20 Preserving Yiddish books and encouraging young people and scholars to study the language and its rich literary output is one aspect of a Jewish cultural revival that is going on in America today.

The Influence of Israel and Zionism

5-21 The German Jews believed in becoming part of the cultural and political life in the United States; the Jewish socialists opposed Zionism on the grounds that it was ethnocentric; some of the Orthodox opposed it because it was primarily a secular rather than religious movement.

5-22 Louis Brandeis, the lawyer and U.S. Supreme Court justice.

5-23 In 1912, Henrietta Szold founded the Jewish women's organization Hadassah to raise money for medical care for Jews in Palestine. In 1918, 2,700 American Jews served in the Jewish Legion under British General Allenby in his liberation of Palestine from the Turks.

5-24 First- and second-generation Jews worried that they would be accused of dual loyalty if they exhibited too much enthusiasm for Zionism. In addition, most of them felt their future lay in America. America was their Zion. Creating a state of Israel, in their view, was a distraction and an illusion.

5-25 It helped to give the communities of the Diaspora a link to Israel and a role in its creation.

5-26 After World War II and the Holocaust, it became clear that a national home for the Jewish people was necessary to safeguard their survival.

5-27 After the Holocaust, support for Israel was a cause on which all Jews could agree. Financial support was critical if Israel were to survive its early years.

5-28 Along with the National Rifle Association and the Cuban lobby, AIPAC is considered the most successful of political lobbies.

Recent Trends

5-29 When Jews moved from cities, they settled in specific suburban towns, where they often made up 20 to 70 percent of the population. Jewish institutions such as synagogues and community centers became a focus of social life even though people drove to them rather than walking as they had in the cities.

5-30 Rabbi Kahane's movement was started to protect elderly Jews in inner-city neighborhoods from random street violence.

5-31 Most non-Orthodox Jewish families now have members of the extended family who are non-Jews. These family members still participate in some family religious celebrations and cultural events.

5-32 There are two opposing trends in the Jewish population. The unaffiliated and intermarried population has grown substantially, but so has the Orthodox and traditional population. There are fewer people in the middle, which accounts for the increasing tension in relationships between the two groups. Whether the Jewish community will survive as one community or will split into separate groups is unclear.

6 POLITICAL PARTICIPATION

▲ Adolf Hitler, the German dictator whose aggressive expansionism sparked World War II, was determined to rid Germany of Jews. Under his regime concentration camps were established, where over six million Jews were killed. By the time Hitler took his own life in April 1945, more than two-thirds of Europe's Jews had been murdered.

Demographic Data

6-1 There are slightly less than six million people who are considered Jews, equal to 2.3 percent of the total population, and 7 million people of Jewish descent (2.7 percent of the total population).

6-2 New York State contains about 28 percent of the Jewish population of America. Nine percent of the state is Jewish.

6-3 Roughly 90 percent. The rest is Sephardi, Middle Eastern, or converts.

6-4 Due to intermarriage and conversion into the Jewish community during the last 30 years in America, a distinctive Jewish look is much less clear today. Today there are black Jews; Asian Jews; and blond-haired, blue-eyed Jews, among others.

6-5 More than 80 percent of American-born Jews were college graduates by the 1980s, and 17 percent of university faculty were of Jewish origin.

6-6 In the song, the Jewish mother worries about and dotes on her children because she knows their life in the outside world will be harsh. In Woody Allen's movies the Jewish mother comes across as a domineering, unsympathetic person who drives her children to neuroses.

6-7 Dr. Ruth Westheimer, Dr. Laura Schlesinger, and sisters Ann Landers (Ask Ann Landers) and Abigail Van Buren (Dear Abby).

Cuisine

6-8 The number of Jews (mainly the Orthodox) buying kosher food has grown in recent years. Also, there are people of other religions (such as Muslims and Seventh Day

Adventists) or strict vegetarians who use kosher certification as a reliable way to follow their dietary requirements.

6-9 Gefilte fish, thick syrupy wine, delicatessen food, kugels (noodle pudding), bagels, and knishes.

6-10 The old New York delis are not popular anymore because this type of food is high in fat and cholesterol and thus a major contributor to heart disease and strokes. Today you can find kosher Chinese, kosher Indian, and kosher sushi, but it's hard to find an old-fashioned kosher deli.

Sectarian Groups

6-11 Lubavitch (or Chabad) from Belarus; Satmar from Hungary;

▼ A "mashgiach" inspects food at a kosher Chinese restaurant in New York City. A mashgiach is a rabbi who ensures that dishes have been prepared according to Jewish dietary laws. Kosher restaurants and prepared foods are a growing part of food industry and production. According to kosher guidelines, milk products and meat should be separated, certain meats such as pork and shellfish should not be eaten, and special rules should be followed when slaughtering animals.

Belz, Ger, and Bobov from Poland; and Vizhnitz from Bukovina (Romania).

6-12 The Lubavitcher Hasidim or the Chabad movement.

6-13 They are extremely insular. They do not watch television or read the secular press, and they still speak Yiddish as their daily language. They also have clung to an anti-Zionist ideology, unlike the other Hasidim.

6-14 When Rabbi Nachman died 200 years ago, they felt he was irreplaceable and thus they have sustained themselves ever since without a rebbe.

6-15 The Bostoner Hasidim led by the Bostoner Rebbe in Brookline, Massachusetts.

Recent Trends

6-16 Jewish liberalism has declined, as has liberalism in the broader society. The secular leadership that dominated Jewish community life for so many generations is gradually being replaced by a more traditional and religiously oriented leadership.

6-17 The main dividing line today is between the more religious and socially conservative Jews and the more liberal and socially assimilated Jews. The same type of division exists in Israel.

6-18 American institutions (such as businesses and universities) are not allowed by law to ask applicants their religion or to discriminate on that basis. Generally the level of social prejudice against Jews in America has gone down to such low levels that it is not a disadvantage to be Jewish.

6-19 This is a symbol of how tolerant and pluralistic America is compared to many other societies. In places such as

Europe and the Middle East, Jews were sometimes forced to convert, but it was exceedingly rare for Christians or Muslims to become Jewish since this would be likely to create disadvantages for or stigmatize them.

6-20 This movement has created stronger personal ties between the Jews of the United States and Israel. Also, the people who move to Israel tend to be ideologically or religiously motivated. Many of them have become leaders in the political and religious movements at both ends of the Israeli political spectrum.

7 CULTURAL LIFE

Yiddish Culture

7-1 Yiddish originated in the 10th or 11th century in the German-speaking lands of Central Europe. The language is based on German, but it contains many Hebrew words and expressions from religious sources as well as influences from Slavic and other languages, including American English.

7-2 It was loved because it contained bits and pieces from all the languages of the societies in which the wandering Jews lived during the last 1,000 years. It was also a uniquely expressive language.

7-3 He was the editor of the largest and most influential Yiddish newspaper, *The Forward*. It played an important role in helping immigrants adapt to American life.

7-4 Isaac Bashevis Singer.

7-5 Singer's father was a rabbi from a shtetl in Poland who wanted his son to become a Talmudic scholar.

7-6 Yiddish writers depicted the wretched plight of working-class Jews struggling to survive in the sweatshops. They also wrote of the generational conflicts between traditional parents and their more secular, Americanized children.

7-7   Sholem Asch, I. J. Singer, Josef Opatoshu, and Peretz Hirschbein.

7-8   The story "Tevye the Milkman," about Jewish life in a shtetl in Eastern Europe, is his most well-known work. This story later became known as *Fiddler on the Roof* in its adaptation as a successful Broadway musical and movie.

7-9   The Orthodox rabbis opposed the Yiddish theater on the grounds that it was frivolous entertainment. The German Jews looked down on it because they considered the plots melodramatic and the Yiddish language a vulgarized form of jargon.

7-10   "Rozhinkes Mit Mandlen."

7-11   By the second generation, Yiddish was no longer the daily language of Jewish Americans, and the Yiddish schools mostly disappeared because the language had no everyday use or religious function.

7-12   Yiddish has been preserved by various Hasidic groups (perhaps 100,000 to 200,000 people) who live mostly in insular neighborhoods in the New York City area. They use it as their daily language.

7-13   Shmaltz, shlock, shlep, kibitz, maven, and klutz are common Yiddish words.

Music

7-14   Irving Berlin (Israel Baline).

7-15   Fanny Brice, George Burns, Eddie Cantor, the Marx brothers.

7-16   *Porgy and Bess.*

7-17   *Rhapsody in Blue* or *An American in Paris.*

7-18 Benny Goodman helped inaugurate the Big Band Era of swing and jazz music in 1934.

7-19 His band was the first one to feature blacks and whites playing together on stage.

7-20 Richard Rodgers and Oscar Hammerstein, and Alan Lerner and Fritz Loewe.

▼ Steven Spielberg's *Schindler's List* was one of the most gripping and disturbing movies about the Holocaust and its effect on humanity. The film chronicles the life of a wealthy German businessman, Oskar Schindler, and his determination to save his 1,100 Jewish employees from certain death in a concentration camp. Spielberg, who is Jewish, is one of the most popular film directors of all time, creating hits like *Raiders of the Lost Ark*, *E.T.*, and *Jurassic Park*.

7-21 *Oklahoma, The Sound of Music,* and *Carousel.*

7-22 *Brigadoon, My Fair Lady,* and *Camelot.*

7-23 Sondheim's shows include *A Funny Thing Happened on the Way to the Forum, Company,* and *Sweeney Todd.* He also wrote the lyrics for the musical *West Side Story.*

7-24 His name is Bob Dylan (formerly Robert Zimmerman). He wrote songs with lyrics critical of contemporary society and laid the basis for the musical part of the 1960s counterculture.

7-25 The conductors were Serge Koussevitzky in Boston, Eugene Ormandy in Philadelphia, Erich Leinsdorf in Cleveland, and Bruno Walter in New York.

7-26 Leonard Bernstein led the New York Philharmonic.

7-27 Itzhak Perlman, Pinchas Zuckerman, Jascha Heifetz, Isaac Stern, and Yehudi Menuhin.

7-28 Aaron Copland.

7-29 Jan Peerce and Richard Tucker.

7-30 Klezmer music is a mixture of religious melodies and lyrics and of Slavic, Turkish, and other Eastern European melodies and rhythms. It has an improvisational style.

7-31 Klezmer bands usually consisted of a clarinetist, a violinist, and a singer. Today, saxophones, guitars, and other band instruments are used.

Comedy

7-32 Borscht Belt humor.

7-33 Danny Kaye, Jerry Lewis, Sid Caesar, Mel Brooks, and Woody Allen.

7-34 These curses are expressed in so clever a way that initially it sounds like they are compliments rather than insults.

Writers

7-35 Undoubtedly it was Gertrude Stein, the daughter of German-Jewish immigrants to America. She had an

▼ Along with his brother, Ira, George Gershwin created the first musical comedy to win the Pulitzer Prize for drama, *Of Thee I Sing*. From the song "Swanee" to the jazz piano concerto *Rhapsody in Blue*, the symphonic poem *An American in Paris*, and the beloved opera *Porgy and Bess*, Gershwin's career covered many types of music, but was cut short when he died suddenly of a brain tumor in 1937. He was only 38.

idiosyncratic style of writing and became famous for her aphorisms ("A rose is a rose is a rose"), her flamboyant lifestyle, and her circle of artistic friends.

7-36 Henry Roth was the author. The novel was unusual in that it was written from the perspective of a little boy and used Yiddish phrases and dialect.

7-37 Henry Roth was criticized by many leftist or radical literary critics when *Call it Sleep* originally came out during the depression years (1930s) for not writing about class conflict. He was a communist sympathizer during those years and took this criticism to heart. More than 50 years passed before he published another book (in 1987).

7-38 Lillian Hellman.

7-39 Saul Bellow, Philip Roth, Bernard Malamud, Joseph Heller, and J. D. Salinger.

7-40 *The Chosen* (which was also made into a movie), *The Promise*, and *My Name is Asher Lev*.

7-41 Cynthia Ozick.

Intellectual Life

7-42 City College of New York earned this title not because of the brilliance of its faculty but rather because of its student body. By the early 20th century, its student population was predominantly second-generation Jews and remained that way for decades. By mid-century, its alumni had earned more Ph.D.'s than those of Harvard (and more Nobel Prizes, as well).

7-43 *Commentary, Partisan Review, Dissent,* and *New York Review of Books*.

7-44 Alfred Kazin.

7-45 Allen Ginsberg became known in the 1950s for his advocacy of spiritual liberation from what he perceived as the standardized culture of the 1950s that valued conformity. He wrote poetry glorifying alternative lifestyles and espousing radical political views.

7-46 *Anne Frank: The Diary of a Young Girl* was published in English in 1952, and *Night*, by Elie Wiesel, was published in English in 1960.

7-47 Like other Americans, many Jewish intellectuals have concluded that many liberal social policies aggravated the problems they were supposed to solve.

Films

7-48 *The Jazz Singer* was an autobiographical film that starred Al Jolson as a cantor's son who becomes a popular jazz singer.

7-49 The novel is *Exodus*. It is about the birth of the state of Israel.

7-50 *Fiddler on the Roof.*

7-51 *Jurassic Park, E.T.*, and *Close Encounters of the Third Kind* are among his popular entertainment movies, and *The Color Purple, Schindler's List*, and *Amistad* are among his more serious films.

7-52 *Love and Death, Annie Hall, Manhattan*, and *Hanna and Her Sisters.*

ANSWERS

CHAPTER

8 POLITICAL PARTICIPATION

Ideological Approaches

8-1 Labor union activity, socialism, communism, Zionism, promotion of Yiddish culture, Reform and Conservative Judaism, Modern Orthodox Judaism, ethical humanism, and civil rights.

8-2 Article VI of the Constitution ensures that no one will be disqualified from public office on the basis of religious affiliation. The First Amendment states that there will be no established (or official) religion in America, unlike in Europe where different denominations of Christianity had the status of national churches. It also guarantees the free exercise of religion to all citizens.

8-3 As a minority that was persecuted by regimes in Europe and the Muslim world and had no voting rights, Jews appreciate the importance of the right to vote. Voting gave them the ability to influence their fate.

8-4 Jewish immigrants began by focusing on economic success in America. Only in the last 30 years have Jews become disproportionately active in political life. This occurred after they had already achieved considerable economic success.

8-5 Democratic candidates received Jewish votes because they supported pro-labor legislation and a more generous welfare state and were more outspoken in their condemnation of racism and anti-Semitism.

8-6 In Russia the main source of anti-Semitic agitation and propaganda had been the Czarist regime and the Russian Orthodox Church. The Communists overthrew the czar and destroyed the power of the church. In America, the Jewish immigrant population was largely made up of working class people who opposed the exploitation of workers that was common in late 19th- and early 20th-century capitalism. Communism and socialism also appealed to a utopian mindset that comes from traditional Judaism.

▼ On March 26, 1979, American President Jimmy Carter participated in the handshake that sealed the Middle East peace treaty between Egypt and Israel. President Anwar Sadat of Egypt and Israeli Prime Minister Menachem Begin ushered in a new era of cooperation, and for the first time in its history Israel had open and peaceful borders with an Arab state.

8-7 Before the 1960s, only people on the political left consistently fought against racial and religious discrimination. In addition, they had as spokesmen many prominent intellectuals and writers. Both of these points appealed to Jews.

8-8 The Jews who were involved in politics during the political machine era (1870–1930) and into the 1960s were active in attempts to reform these political machines out of existence. They believed it was more important to build a better welfare state than to have a smoothly functioning but corrupt machine running city government.

World War II and the Holocaust

8-9 Father Coughlin, a Roman Catholic priest.

8-10 Henry Ford and Charles Lindbergh.

8-11 President Roosevelt supported the liberal social and economic policies that most Jews supported and was a staunch advocate of fighting Nazism when others supported an isolationist (neutral) policy.

8-12 Many members of the American political elite have felt a special responsibility to support Israel's security needs as a compensation for American indifference to the victims of the Holocaust before and during World War II.

Politics and the State of Israel

8-13 Eddie Jacobson, an old Jewish friend of President Truman's from Independence, Missouri, had been a business partner with Truman before he went into politics. He encouraged the president to meet Chaim Weizmann. Weizmann was the head of the Zionist movement and later became the first president of Israel. Apparently Truman was impressed with Weizmann and his arguments. This meeting influenced his decision.

8-14 The war marked the emergence of Israel as a self-confident military power in the region. Prior to 1967, Israel was portrayed in America as an object of charity and a weak country surrounded by powerful neighbors. After the war it was no longer seen as the underdog.

8-15 The war caused a revival of Orthodox Judaism in Israel and the Diaspora and a rise in militant and messianic fringe groups among the Orthodox in both Israel and America.

▼ In a 1909 demonstration, two young socialists carry banners bearing identical slogans in Yiddish and in English. The Jewish passion for political, as well as personal, freedom can be traced back to the time of Moses and the founding doctrine of Judaism: "Man is more than property; even to his master he gives only his service. His person is free."

8-16 It signified how the military victory and subsequent reunification of Jerusalem struck a chord of exhilaration and unity among American Jews. Even those Jews far removed from participation in community life, such as many Jews in the entertainment industry, were moved by the great victory.

8-17 President Jimmy Carter of the U.S., President Anwar Sadat of Egypt, and Prime Minister Menachem Begin of Israel.

8-18 This period coincided with the rise of right-wing political parties in Israel and neo-conservative forces within the American Jewish community.

8-19 Jewish philanthropy from the Diaspora was estimated to be about one billion dollars per year during the 1980s. Two-thirds of this amount came from American Jews.

8-20 The ceremony, organized by President Bill Clinton, was held on the White House lawn.

Contemporary Politics and Issues

8-21 When the civil rights movement of the 1960s evolved into a Black Power movement, Jewish supporters, along with many other sympathetic whites, began to abandon it. The anti-Semitic remarks of some African-American public figures in recent years has also served to weaken the bonds between the two groups.

8-22 Affirmative action in its early years was portrayed as an attempt to help minorities overcome institutional discrimination in hiring and university admission. As time went by, affirmative action policies became more like quotas. Historically Jews have many negative experiences with quotas both in Europe and America, where it has been used as a way to limit the entrance of qualified Jewish candidates to higher education or professional positions.

8-23 Abbie Hoffman and Jerry Rubin. Rubin became a Wall Street investment specialist and Hoffman continued with his activism until he committed suicide in the 1980s.

8-24 Noam Chomsky (MIT) and Herbert Marcuse (Brandeis) were among the radical academics who were outspoken in their opposition to the Vietnam War and what they saw as the racist social system of the United States.

8-25 Neo-conservatives claimed that contemporary liberalism blamed too many of society's problems on impersonal forces ("the system") rather than on the breakdown of individual responsibility and morality.

8-26 Incumbent Republican mayor Rudy Giuliani defeated his liberal Democratic challenger, Ruth Messinger, and won 76 percent of the Jewish vote, which provided him with his margin of victory. Twenty years ago, the Jewish vote would have gone the other way.

8-27 Recently Jewish congressmen have represented districts in states such as Kansas, and Jewish senators have represented states such as Minnesota, Connecticut, and Nevada. None of these states or districts have large Jewish populations. This means the Jewish candidates are being elected overwhelmingly by gentile voters.

9 IMPORTANT PERSONALITIES and PEOPLE OF ACCOMPLISHMENT

Intellectual and Cultural Figures

9-1   J. Robert Oppenheimer.

9-2   Erich Fromm.

9-3   Walter Lippmann.

9-4   Louis Brandeis, the son of German-Jewish immigrants, was appointed by President Woodrow Wilson in 1916. His appointment was opposed both by anti-Semitic forces and by big business, which thought he was too concerned with worker's rights.

9-5   The Vizhnitz Hasidim.

9-6   He wrote a devastating critique of the system of American medical education before World War I and gave recommendations on how to improve it. By the end of World War II, American medical education was the best in the world.

9-7   He is considered the father of the American hydrogen bomb and was a strong supporter of Ronald Reagan's Star Wars project.

9-8   Ben Shahn, Mark Rothko, Louse Nevelson, and Max Weber.

▲ The two atomic bombs dropped on Japan in August 1945 forced that country to stop waging World War II against the United States and its allies. Hundreds of the world's most talented scientists and engineers worked on the "Manhattan Project" to develop the atom bomb. A Jewish-American physicist, Dr. J. Robert Oppenheimer, was the director of the Manhattan Project.

◀ Larry Bird was probably one of the best-known members of the National Basketball Association's Boston Celtics. Arnold "Red" Auerbach, a Jewish American, made the team one of the most successful in the NBA as both a coach (1950–66) and as general manager (1966–94). As a coach, he won 1,037 games and nine NBA titles.

Political Leaders and Public Figures

9-9 Haym Solomon, who had gained experience as a currency broker in his native Poland as well.

9-10 Herbert Lehman was elected in 1932 on the Democratic ticket. He came from the famous banking family of German Jews.

9-11 LaGuardia's father was an Italian Catholic and his mother a Jew. He converted to the Episcopal Church as an adult. He spoke fluent English, Italian, and Yiddish and used all three languages in his political campaigns.

9-12 Edward Koch was mayor from 1977–89. He is now a columnist and radio commentator.

9-13 Barry Goldwater ran for president in 1964. His father came from a Jewish family.

9-14 The three accomplishments were 1) arranging the cease-fire after the Yom Kippur War between Israel and the Arabs; 2) negotiating an end to the Vietnam War and winning the Nobel Peace Prize for that effort; and 3) contributing significantly to the process of reestablishing U.S. relations with communist China.

9-15 Her parents were Czech Jews who converted to Catholicism after Czechoslovakia was invaded by the Nazis.

Entertainment and Sports

9-16 Acting in Broadway and Hollywood musicals, directing and producing movies, and singing popular music.

9-17 Hank Greenberg, Sandy Koufax, and Al Rosen.

9-18 He refused to pitch on Yom Kippur, the most sacred day in the Jewish calendar, and was rescheduled to pitch on another day.

9-19 Mark Spitz, a swimmer, won seven gold medals in the 1972 Olympics.

9-20 Arnold "Red" Auerbach as the coach of the Boston Celtics had the highest winning percentage of any NBA coach.

Military Service

9-21 Commodore Uriah P. Levy, who fought in the War of 1812.

9-22 Hyman Rickover. He was nicknamed the "Father of the nuclear navy" because he introduced the first nuclear-powered submarine into navy service.

Activists

9-23 Emma Lazarus wrote the poem that begins, "Give me your tired, your poor, your huddled masses yearning to breathe free," in 1889.

9-24 Emma Goldman.

▼ Mission specialist Judith A. Resnick (third from left) was a member of the crew of the doomed space shuttle Challenger. Millions of Americans watched, shocked, as Challenger exploded two minutes after lifting off in 1986. Resnick, who received her Ph.D. in electrical engineering and joined NASA's space program in 1978, had been the second American woman to travel in space. The Society of Women Engineers has named an award in her honor.

9-25 Samuel Gompers, a Jewish immigrant from England, became the AFL's first president in 1886. Unlike many of the early union leaders who favored radical actions and promoted socialism or communism, Gompers focused on improving conditions for the workers within the existing system.

9-26 Golda Meir was born in Russia in 1898 and emigrated with her family to Milwaukee, Wisconsin, in 1906. She emigrated to Israel in 1921.

9-27 In the 1980s, he worked for U.S. Naval Intelligence and passed classified information to Israeli intelligence.

Further Reading

Barnavi, Eli (editor). *A Historical Atlas of the Jewish People.* London: Hutchinson, 1992.

Donin, Hayim Halevy. *To Be A Jew: A Guide to Jewish Observance in Contemporary Life.* New York: Basic Books, 1991.

Halkin, Hillel. *Letters to an American Jewish Friend, A Zionist's Polemic.* Philadelphia: Jewish Publication Society, 1977.

Hertzberg, Arthur. *The Jews in America: Four Centuries of an Uneasy Counter.* New York: Simon and Schuster, 1989.

Howe, Irving. *World of Our Fathers.* New York and London: Harcourt Brace Jovanovich, 1976.

Moore, Deborah Dash. *To the Golden Cities: Pursuing the American Jewish Dream to Miami and LA.* New York: Free Press, 1994.

Muggamin, Howard, *The Jewish Americans.* New York: Chelsea House Publishers, 1996.

Lipset, Seymour Martin and Earl Raab. *The Jews and the New American Scene.* Cambridge: Harvard University Press, 1996.

O'Brien, Conor Cruise. *The Siege: The Saga of Israel and Zionism.* New York: Simon and Schuster, 1986.

Sachar, Howard. *A History of the Jews in America.* New York: Alfred A. Knopf, 1992.

Thernstrom, Stephen, Ann Orlov, and Oscar Handlin (editors). *Harvard Encyclopedia of American Ethnic Groups.* Cambridge: The Belknap Press, Harvard University Press, 1980.

Index

Index

Index

Index

*Page numbers in **bold** indicate photos and their captions*

Picture Credits

About the Contributors

General Editor SANDRA STOTSKY is director of the Institute on Writing, Reading, and Civic Education at the Harvard Graduate School of Education as well as a research associate there. She served as editor of *Research in the Teaching of English,* a journal sponsored by the National Council of Teachers of English, from 1991–97.

Dr. Stotsky holds a bachelor of arts degree with distinction from the University of Michigan and a doctorate in education from the Harvard Graduate School of Education. She has taught on the elementary and high school levels and at Northeastern University, Curry College, and the Harvard Graduate School of Education. Her work in education has ranged from serving on academic advisory boards to developing elementary and secondary civics curricula as a consultant to American, Polish, Lithuanian, and Romanian educators. She has written numerous scholarly articles, curricular materials, encyclopedia entries, and reviews, and is the author of three books on education.

General Editor REED UEDA is associate professor of history at Tufts University. He graduated summa cum laude with a bachelor of arts degree from UCLA, received master of arts degrees from both the University of Chicago and Harvard University, and received a doctorate from Harvard.

Dr. Ueda was research editor of the *Harvard Ethnic Encyclopedia of America* and has served on the board of editors for *American Quarterly, Harvard Educational Review, Journal of Interdisciplinary History,* and *University of Chicago School Review.* He is the author or coauthor of several books on ethnic studies, including *Postwar Immigrant America: A Social History, Ethnic Groups in History Textbooks,* and *Immigration.*

ELLEN SHNIDMAN has written articles and essays on social issues for a number of journals. She has also coauthored articles on the social and biological sciences. She graduated magna cum laude from Yale University and earned a master of science degree from the Weizmann Institute of Science in Israel. She lives in Rochester, New York.